A Sparrow Sings

Lynda Shelhamer
John Shelhamer

D1472694

He put a new song in my mouth, a song of praise to our God; Many will see and fear and will trust in the Lord.

Psalm 40:3

Dedicated to:

Josiah Wesley Shelhamer.

Whose death defined the rest of my life in so many ways.

I miss smelling your softness, feeling the tears that you were
unable to cry, groping for the answers to your deep and difficult
questions and … cuddling till you laughed … cuddling …

Thank you for sharing your song.

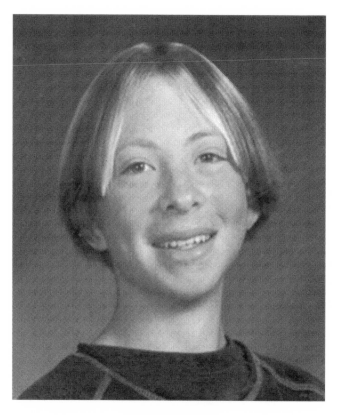

1983-1998

I wish th at I cood go too hevin nou! right

- Josiah age 5

Josiah's Special Message

As a Hospice Nurse I've been at the bedside of many a dying patient. I can attest that the moment of death is not as painful as most of us imagine and that it is not uncommon for the passing one to see heaven, Jesus or others who have passed before them.

Such was my Josiah's experience. I believe God gave him the strength to write about it and me the privilege to share with fellow grieving parents. In the Scriptures Jesus promises to be with us even to the end of the earth. And so He is!!

Josiah completed his life using a 22 Rifle, the coroner felt that there was a 15 minute period between the time the gun went off and the time he passed. This explains why the blood stained note is misspelled, with words missing and looks like a child's writing not a 15year olds.

His message is this: God is Mighty, God is Loving and very importantly God is Our Father. Without the later the first two would be nice but not significant to a dying person!

Like a newborn struggling it's way out of a dark, confining womb there can be freedom and new air on the "other side."

"Free at last thank God I free……"

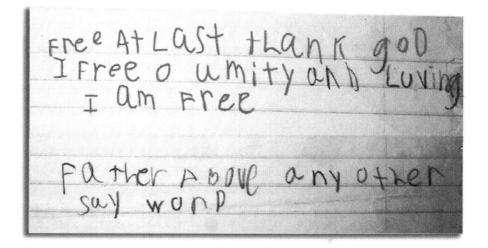

Contents

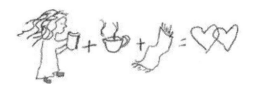

Introduction

A bird hits the window. You stare at its seemingly lifeless body and wonder … is it dead? Will it ever move, fly or sing again?

Some birds do and some birds don't!

Maybe, just maybe, this one will sing again! Maybe, just maybe, mom, you will sing again.

When my little bird, Josiah, hit the window he bypassed the hard ground and flew right through the Window of Heaven, never to fly again on this beautiful planet. I, on the other hand, slammed hard against the dark pane of death, lying stunned on the cold earth below believing I would never fly or sing again.

A Sparrow Falls was about your dirge, your lament. Guiding you to take those first breaths and learning to croak out a "good day."

A Sparrow Sings is designed to allow your Composer/Conductor God to instill a new song into your sorrow.

Grieving the loss of a child and finding one's voice again can feel like a long laborious journey. But be encouraged mom, the God who taught the stars to sing (Job 38:7), and me to sing again can create in you a new song. In discovering and practicing your new song you will find your voice and sing again!! I have a choir of moms to prove it! So grab your favorite cozy wrap, cup of coffee and prepare to become a composer, learning to sing again!

Each devotional will guide you into:

• A Sonnet from God's heart and My heart

• A Composing Section intended as a discovery dialogue between you and your Conductor

• A Selah your musical interlude, your pause for the day, and for our purposes an affirmation.

What about the male bird? Will he sing again? In the second section of this devotional my wonderful husband and co-conductor of our life song, John, has included devotionals from his song. This is intended as a "dad read" but feel free moms to take a peek.

Your Canon is Calling

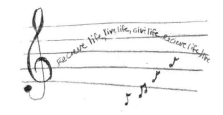

"My heart is steadfast, I will make music with all my soul."
Psalm 108:1

A Canon, by definition, is a melody that is repeated as an underlying theme throughout a song.

For our purposes, it is a melody that will be repeated within your *life song* or in today's vernacular, your "mission and purpose statement."

After Josiah passed we didn't want to lose our passion for living. Our purpose had become a blurred, soiled heap on the floor of our grieving lives. We prayed for a new canon that would help us regain focus and trade our *sympathy* for a *symphony,* our *sorrow* for a *song.*

The Heavenly Songwriter gave us the title: "Receive Life, Live Life, and Give Life."

This frequently repeated melody has helped John and me make decisions and sing our new song more clearly.

There are "stanzas" in life when we are physically and emotionally drained, calling for our **Receive Life** melody. During these times, we will go off alone or call on prayer warrior friends to pray for us. We spend time on our knees and in God's Word… receiving life.

My **Live Life** melody is a daily hike but it is a run up the mountain for John. It's game nights with friends and vacations with family and grandchildren.

Our **Give Life** stanzas include facilitating GriefShare, Bible studies, support groups, conferences for grieving moms, and sharing my Juice Plus, plant-based products.

Our life decisions are based on our Canon which helps our *life song* to be sung well! When we get off-key, which of course happens, it is usually because we've lost sight of our Canon.

Your Composition

Discovery Dialog with your Composer: Begin opening your heart to the idea of a *Life Canon* it will give intent to your days, and provide a steadfast refrain when life notes soar to a high soprano or plummet to a low base.

What are we instructed to do with our song? Deuteronomy 31:19.

Prayer: Ask the Lord today for a *Life Canon.* If this is too complicated, go ahead and steal ours.

Selah: I will say "yes" to what aligns with my life song and "no" to what doesn't.

_____
_____
_____
_____
_____
_____
_____
_____
_____
_____

Elementary Lessons

Fixing our eyes on Jesus the Author and Finisher of our faith.
Hebrews 12:2

Okay, who else took two years of piano lessons then quit? I know I wasn't alone in this childhood "take lessons in everything" stage of life! With the red, John Thompson's: First Grade book propped on my piano, I'd proudly play my three-note song: "Here we go, up a road, to a birthday party." I can still play it on my air piano using just three fingers. John Thompson's book is still out there on Amazon, and it's still big and red!

This rudimentary practice required three elements: a book, a teacher, and a willingness to practice. The last is where my piano career failed. I never had *the will* to practice, well, with the exception being the hour before my dreaded lesson.

Our Composer not only writes but finishes our song. He hands us the Book (our Bible) and provides the teacher (the Holy Spirit), and, drum roll please, gives us the *will* to practice!

Philippians 2:13, God is working in you both to *will* and to do for His good pleasure.

Some of you may have only an inkling of what your **new song** might be. Some of you may be totally clueless.

Start by practicing - three simple steps: try something, practice it, and God will give you *the will*. Your song will come!

I love that I don't need to worry about how to write and finish my **new song**. This verse says that He is the Author (composer) and Finisher of our faith! Hallelujah! He has composed the beginning, the middle, and the ending of your song, let Him teach it to you!

Your Composition

Discovery Dialog with your Composer: Who has equipped you to play your new song? Hebrews 13:20-21.

Prayer: Father, Composer of everything that's beautiful in this world, You taught the stars to sing - share with me a **new song** and give me *the will* to practice it.

Selah: This year, I'm expecting God to give me a new song, and *the will* to practice it.

_____
_____
_____
_____
_____
_____
_____
_____
_____
_____
_____
_____
_____
_____
_____
_____
_____
_____
_____
_____
_____
_____
_____

The Sacred Stick

Aaron's rod had not only sprouted, but it had budded, blossomed, and produced almonds.
Numbers 17:8

As a child, I heard about Aaron's rod in Sunday school; the rod that was so special it was placed in the Ark of the Covenant. I also heard about Moses's rod that became a snake, and a Russian fairy tale about a stick that came alive and chased a goat! My young mind mixed these together and I thought it was Aaron's rod that "butted" like a goat (not "budded")!

As an adult, I was curious about the real story and went to Numbers 17.

Moses was overwhelmed with all his responsibilities and he needed to choose a priest to assist with spiritual issues. It was declared the head of each of the 12 family households was to bring a dead stick into the Tent of Meeting, the sacred space where God met with man while in the desert. In a very short time, Aaron's dead-stick sprouted, then budded, blossomed, and brought forth fruit!

Our Tent of Meeting is that sacred spot where we daily meet with God. My meeting place is in the morning on my bed. Propped up with pillows, the sun beginning to stream in, my Bible and journal on my lap, and a cup of tea close at hand, I share communion with Him.

We've all been handed a dead branch, the loss of our child. We can sit and stare at it for years or we can drag our branch into the Tent of Meeting and allow the presence of God to make a miracle happen - bringing my dead stick back to life - sprouting, budding, blossoming, and finally bringing forth fruit.

I dragged mine to God and He gave me the desire to write a devotional for grieving moms. The idea was the sprout. The rough draft was the bud. The completed draft the blossom. And finally (okay, ten "finales"), a book.

Your fruit might be something totally different than mine. Are you willing to drag your dead stick to the Tent of Meeting after your cold, dark, winter and watch it sprout?

Your "blossom" may be inviting a fellow grieving mom out to lunch or a hike. It's a start. My daughter-in-law, Whitney, married my son, Zak, in an almond grove. Fragrant pink petals played in the gentle breeze and lined the dirt path as they exchanged their covenant vows.

Imagine it! Your small almond bud could someday become a fragrant, blossoming grove! Miracles do happen in the Tent of Meeting.

Discovery Dialog with your Composer: What did God show Jeremiah, and what did it symbolize? Jeremiah 1:11,12.

Prayer: Lord, show me a small sprout of new life today, renew my hope for a miracle.

Selah: I will thank God for the new life He is giving my dead branch.

_____

_____

_____

 *Tale of Two Trees*

In the middle of the garden were the Tree of Life and the Tree of the Knowledge of Good and Evil.
Genesis 2:9

Two trees stood grandly in the fauna and flora of the Garden of Eden; both laden with fruit and attractive to the eye.

As God fellowshipped with Adam along the sun bathed paths, He explained: eat freely of the trees, they are life for you and for Eve. However, don't touch or consume the fruit of the Tree of the Knowledge of Good and Evil it is deadly. Stop! Make a different choice, its fruit is poison!

The fruit of this later tree is still poison! It will kill your creative genes quicker than anything as you weigh the heavy knowledge of "Am I good or am I evil?" This constant self-reflection of one's own goodness or badness will consume your mind and result in either spiritual pride "good," or shame, blame, guilt and judgment, "evil." Stop! Make a different choice, redirect your attention to the Tree of Life.

The Tree of Life represents Calvary. Its fruit is eternal and when we stretch out our hands and partake of its Life-Fruit, we live eternally (I John 5:11-13). The shame, blame, judgment tree was destroyed by Jesus as He bore all of that mess for us on the cross. This tree is never mentioned again in the Scriptures, however, the Tree of Life is eternal and is mentioned as casting its shadow over the River of Life in the midst of heaven. This time it is no longer healing individuals but entire nations (Revelation 22).

If you have been focusing on the wrong tree, I want to invite you to the Tree of Life. Reach out, taste and see that its fruit is good! The shadow cast over you will not be one of "good or evil" but rather Christ's righteousness and the life you have in Him.

Your Composition

Discovery Dialog with your Composer: Have you eaten of the tree of life? If so what is the result? I John 5:11-12

Prayer: Lord, thank you for taking the shame, blame, and judgment of my sin and destroying it on Calvary. I receive your eternal life as my own.

Selah: Today, I am singing with gratitude in my heart for the tree of life.

_____
_____
_____
_____
_____
_____
_____
_____
_____
_____
_____
_____
_____
_____
_____
_____
_____
_____
_____
_____
_____
_____
_____

Completing the Uncompleted

For there is hope for a tree when it is cut down that it will sprout again and it's roots will not fail.
Job 14:7.

Hebrews 11 has been referred to as the "Hall of Faith," as one saint after another is showcased for *believing* God and *received* what He promised them. Noah r*eceived* the salvation of his family via the Ark. Abraham and Sarah *received* their promised child. Moses *received* deliverance for His people. Even Rahab the harlot r*eceived* salvation for herself and her family. The beat goes on - saints with great faith r*eceiving* the promises for which they *believed*.

However, in verses 36-40, the tempo changes. The list turns to others, like our children, who had lives seemingly cut short: martyrs, misfits, desert mountain wanderers, and cave dwellers. People who somehow, didn't make the big hero list, and "...died *without receiving* what was promised."

My son, Josiah, fell into this category as he was somewhat of a misfit. He was definitely a wanderer whose life was, by the world's standards, cut short.

I love the explanation as to why this could happen in the verses that follow: Because God provided something better for us, (you and me mom) that together with us, they could be made complete.

Can I really be a part of completing a life that was seemingly cut short? Can I honor Josiah's life by helping complete it here on earth? I believe I can! I believe we can!

The world's first family lost their youngest son, his life cut short by murder. In the same chapter of Hebrews, referring to Abel, it says "through faith, though he is dead, he still speaks." Abel lived and died some 6,000 -10,000 years ago. His story <u>still</u> gives him a voice. I want Josiah's death to have meaning, to have a voice. So I sing his song through Heavenly Hope and Healing, and through random acts of kindness and faith.

Your Composition

Discovery Dialog with your Composer: What does Paul say he is doing in regards to Christ's afflictions? Colossians 1:24.

Prayer: Lord, thank you that I have been given the opportunity to sing my child's song for him/her. Show me a way to redeem and multiply the good within him/her.

Selah: My child's song is being infused into my soul, giving greater purpose, greater joy, and creating greater good in my world.

_____
_____
_____
_____
_____
_____
_____
_____
_____
_____
_____
_____
_____
_____
_____

Mountain Top Experience

And in the daytime He was teaching in the temple, but at night He
went out and stayed on the mount called Olivet.
Luke 21:37.

Jesus often went into the *mountains* to pray, sleep and teach.

In the Bible, significant events almost always took place on *mountains*. Check it out: Noah's ark rested on *Mount* Ararat; the Law was given on *Mount* Sinai; Moses's burning bush experience was on *Mount* Horeb; Elijah defeated Jezebel and Baal on *Mount* Carmel; Jesus's Beatitudes are called "The Sermon on the *Mount*;" Jesus struggled in the garden on the *Mount* of Olives; He was transfigured on *Mount* Hermon, and was crucified on *Mount* Calvary. Maybe it's because I live in the *mountains* that I notice this.

You may not have access to a *mountain*, but you do have access to the questions God asked people on the *mountains*. Did you ever notice that the God of the Bible is really the only God/god who reasons with His people? He even told Isaiah, "come, let us reason together." Most gods are portrayed as being fierce and made to be revered, not to be reasoned with or questioned, but not our God.

On *Mount* Horeb, God asked Moses, "what's in your hand?" This is also where He asked Elijah, "What are you doing here?" It's not like God didn't know the answers to these questions but he wanted man to explore the answers for themselves. These are two very significant questions we can allow God to ask us today as we stand on the peak of life.

For years after my son's death, I asked God, "What are **You** doing here?" Like Elijah in this story, after the earthquake, fire, and whirlwind, I finally heard God's still small voice asking *me*, "what are you doing here?" Exploring the answer to these two questions began my song.

Moses's answer to God's question "what's in your hand?" seemed obvious; a staff. But God used that common staff to part the Red Sea, bring water out of a rock, and free the children of Israel.

Today, go somewhere free of distraction and allow God to ask you these two questions: "What are you doing here?" and "What's in your hand?" Look past the obvious and reason with the God of the Universe.

Discovery Dialog with your Composer: Read this passage in its entirety and answer the question, "what are you doing here?" Feel free to voice your complaint as Elijah did. I Kings 19:9-14.

Prayer: Lord, You've shared gifts, talents and life experiences with me. Show me what's "in my hand" that I may use to honor You and help others.

Selah: I will use "what's in my hand" today to glorify You.

_____
_____
_____
_____
_____
_____
_____
_____
_____
_____
_____

Flying Lesson

Behold one shall fly like an eagle...
Jeremiah 48:40

Every kid I grew up with wanted to fly like Superman. My brothers and I would pin towels to our backs, climb up on the fireplace mantle and jump from the mantel to the back of the highest chair, our towel capes flying through the air. Even now, in my reoccurring dreams, I'm often flying or watching something fly and I flap my arms vigorously until I'm on the ceiling ...

Flying, however, is not all that easy. A mother eagle will take her precious egret high in the air and drop him. Frightened and seemingly abandoned, he plummets toward the earth, stretching out his wings as he flies awkwardly toward the hard earth.

When Josiah died I felt I had been "dropped" by God. I felt frightened, confused, and abandoned as I plummeted to the hard earth.

The mommy eagle will keep doing this until the egret discovers that which was already built in him from birth: he can fly! He discovered something in him that was there from birth!

I still have days of confused abandonment, but I am discovering my spiritual DNA, my song, with each attempt at flying. Admittedly, I frequently have to push myself off the cliff but I always take the leap!

Spread your wings mom. I know you have that "something" in you that you will discover, even if it feels awkward at first, spread your broken wings.

The other fact I love about eagles is that, unlike crows and turkey vultures, they never feed on dead food or garbage. An eagle will only eat living food! If we are going to nourish our flying wings we need to feed on the living Word of God - Manna from heaven, not earth's garbage!

Discovery Dialog with your Composer: What is God's promise for those who "wait on the Lord?" Isaiah 40:31

Prayer: Give me the courage to jump off the scary life cliffs and learn to fly again.

Selah: I enjoy a diet of God's word over the easily accessible garbage of the world.

_____
_____
_____
_____
_____
_____
_____
_____
_____
_____
_____
_____
_____
_____
_____
_____
_____

Who Told You That You Were Naked?

And He said, "Who told you that you were naked? Have you eaten
from the tree of which I commanded that you should not eat?"
Genesis 3:11

You and I, moms, live in a "not enough" world. Advertisements are targeted to make us feel that we are drastically lacking, so that we desperately need their offer or their product.

We've been bombarded with this "not enough" message since grade school. Gifted programs made us feel not gifted, so did picking teams for games or sports. Fellow students were ingenious at finding and taking advantage of our Achilles Heel. My maiden name was Wesley, so I quickly was labeled Wesson Oil, "fat in the can." I didn't know my can was fat until they told me! "Who told you?" John, being a Shelhamer, was quickly changed to Sledge Hammer then, shortened to Sludge.

Adam and Eve discovered their nakedness when the ultimate bully coerced them into eating of the death tree. Immediately a voice entered their heads "am I good or bad?" Just as quickly as the thought came, they concluded "I am bad, I'm naked!," and becoming afraid, hid themselves.

In our nakedness we hide so no one will notice our "not enough-ness." We cannot sing our *New Song* if we are afraid it will be off-key. Worse yet we may be afraid God is finding us "not enough," or that our fellow-earthlings will deem us "not enough."

Who told you? The voice is loud in our heads - worse than the school yard bullies, we have become or own bully. Paul so clearly betrays this struggle in Romans 7. Finally the voice in his head shouts out in verse 34, "there is no condemnation for those in Christ Jesus!"

God saw Adam and Eve in distress over their nakedness, slew an animal, and made a skin covering for them. This symbolized the day when His own Son would be slain and His blood would cover our "not enough-ness," and completely dissipate it.

We now stand in white clothes of royalty - fully "enough" in Christ! Enough for everything! So instead of singing while no one is listening, bellow your song like everyone is listening. You are God's Diva! <u>You are enough</u> to sing any song He gives you!

Discovery Dialog with your Composer: In what areas are you repeatedly telling yourself "I am not enough?" What does this verse tell you about your "enough-ness?" Colossians 2:10.

Prayer: Lord, open my eyes to the world's lies that I am naked-not enough. Show me your adequacy and sufficiency for all things.

Selah: I am equipped and enough for every task I am facing today.

_____
_____
_____
_____
_____
_____
_____
_____
_____
_____

Unwrapping the Grave Clothes

Jesus said to them, 'unbind him and let him go.'
John 11:44

No one at Lazarus's funeral wanted the stone to be rolled away from the tomb, much less unwrap his grave clothes - because, they said, it would stink (John 11:39)!

Death stinks. Everything about it stinks. It totally stinks that my son and your child died!

As a hospice nurse, I came to know the "smell of death" even before one dies. Lazarus had been dead for four days when Jesus approached the tomb. Did Jesus wait to make sure he was not just dead, but good and dead, so people would not doubt the miracle? Was He giving Mary and Martha time to grieve? Those faithful gatherers believed Jesus could have healed him. The sisters affirmed, "If You were here …" and "If you had gotten here sooner …" he would have lived.

Jesus wept with them despite knowing he was going to resurrect Lazarus. I believe He wept with us knowing He was going to resurrect our child. After all, He's labeled The Man of Sorrows, acquainted with grief (Isaiah 53).

There comes a time, however, when He says to us too, "unbind him and let him go!" In Matthew 19:14 Jesus says,".. *suffer* the children to come to Me, for such is the Kingdom of Heaven."

You may not be ready to completely unravel the grave clothes and set your child free, but what if, just what if, you do, and instead of it stinking, a beautiful aroma for Christ diffuses. Lazarus's aroma certainly did! The release of Lazarus brought crowds of followers to Jesus (John 12:9) and became a testimony to the world!

Discovery Dialog with your Composer: What does this say about the aroma of death versus the aroma of life? 2 Corinthians 2:16.

Prayer: Lord, give me the strength to unravel my child's grave clothes one strip at a time, releasing an aroma of life.

Selah: I will allow my child to become an "aroma of life" to others.

_____
_____
_____
_____
_____
_____
_____
_____
_____
_____
_____
_____
_____
_____
_____
_____
_____
_____
_____
_____
_____

My China Cabinet

Now in a large house there are not only gold and silver vessels, but also vessels of wood and earthenware. Some to honor and some to dishonor.
2 Timothy 2:20

Loving to entertain, I have cabinets of shelves laden with dishes (much to the chagrin of my children who have to go through it all someday).

I'm ready for any occasion! Being Swedish I have the fine china for holidays and teas but I also have everyday dishes. Party dishes, plastic and paper plates for outdoor events, dog bowls for when the pups arrive, even an ashtray for my smoking friends. Vessels of honor to be carefully handled, polished and put back on the shelf. Some for dishonor, to be trashed, or have the ashes washed off.

Timothy explains to us that God also has all these vessels in His house of believers (church). Each of us gets to choose what kind of vessel we will be. According to verse 21, the honorable vessel cleanses himself according to the Word and becomes sanctified, or set apart, for the Master's use. Prepared for every good work.

Earlier in the chapter, Timothy gives us three additional keys to being a vessel of honor. I call it the "Rub-a-dub-dub Three Men in a Tub" example. However, instead of the Butcher, the Baker, and the Candle Stick Maker, it's the Soldier, the Athlete, and the Farmer.

The soldier suffers hardship ("check," we've done that) but does not entangle himself in the affairs of this world (a bit harder!). The athlete focuses on the prize and sticks to the rules of the game. The farmer works hard and gets to share in the harvest.

I don't want to be an ashtray or a discarded, soiled paper plate. I want to be a vessel of honor so that God can take me off the shelf and serve royalty … or better yet, a picnic lunch on the beach with family and friends. According to Timothy, we get to make that choice.

 *Your Composition*

Discovery Dialog with your Composer: Which of these three keys can you use to sanctify your vessel? 2 Timothy 2:3-6.

Prayer: I lift my cup up to You today to be used as You chose.

Selah: Daily, I offer my vessel to be used by the Master.

_____
_____
_____
_____
_____
_____
_____
_____
_____
_____
_____
_____
_____
_____
_____

Your Seed's Potential

Truly, truly, I say to you, unless a grain of wheat falls into the earth and dies, it remains alone; but if it dies, it bears much fruit.
John 12:24

Parable? Riddle? A dead seed, fallen into the cold earth produces much fruit!

Our kids loved reading *Frog and Toad* books. One particular adventure found Frog and Toad planting and watering some seeds in their backyard. Anticipation was followed by discouragement, however, as they daily checked on their seeds and found nothing but black dirt! Finally one day a small green sprout of hope appeared...

The seed of your child's death can produce an entire field of grain! Staring at the black earth, feeling that sense of anticipation continually eclipsed by disappointment, you might find this hard to imagine. But I've seen it happen over and over again.

Tears water our seed. God adds His Son-shine and *with time*, miracles happen.

Everyone's crop will appear unique, but the essence of grain is that it nourishes someone!

A great example of a seed coming to harvest are our friends, The Moritz's, started Breanna's House of Joy for orphaned girls in Thailand in honor of their precious Breanna Joy, who was killed in a car accident. Other moms have formed anti-bullying groups and one started a lifeguard awareness group to prevent future drownings. Another opened a ranch for girls who were sex trafficked. My hiking friend, Chris, who lost her two children, went on to become a Stephen Minister and now volunteers at a home for Alzheimer patients.

Your crop doesn't have to be huge like theirs. It could be as simple as helping with GriefShare, or taking another hurting mom to coffee... and I'm just saying, sometimes our own seed needs to die to self in order to become fruitful.

Your Composition

Discovery Dialog with your Composer: Who tends our seed in the dark ground? What does He do with it? I Corinthians 15:36-38.

Prayer: As I stare at my buried seed, watering it with my tears, bring new life, Lord.

Selah: I believe the Master Gardener is bringing life to my seed.

_____
_____
_____
_____
_____
_____
_____
_____
_____
_____
_____
_____
_____
_____
_____
_____
_____
_____

Rattled

For I know nothing good dwells in me, for the willing is present in me but the doing of good is not.
Romans 7:18

True confession time: I've always been somewhat of a spiritual outlaw. I can identify with the beach sign: "Work like a Captain, *Play like a Pirate.*"

Growing up in a conservative, Christian home, I definitely found a thrill in pushing the limits. In Bible College, the Dean explained that he didn't think I was bad, (thank goodness!) I was just "mischievous." I once had to work off my "demerits" by cleaning chairs late into the night to avoid expulsion. The Bible talks about a "spirit of lawlessness" and I always feared I had a touch of that virus!

However, God gave this disciple a lesson in playing in the grey areas through a coiled rattlesnake. Each year snake bites are the source of 81,000 deaths worldwide. Chris, my grieving-mom hiking-buddy, and I have hiked daily in the Garden of the Gods for five years. Warning signs about rattlesnakes line the marked paths but though we have seen rattlesnakes we've never had a serious encounter with one.

Until – one particular warm spring morning when I was on a trail I wasn't supposed to be on, hunting wild asparagus I wasn't supposed to be picking. (I justify this by telling myself that asparagus is more sustainable if picked!)

With my eyes focused across the field for the tell-tale sign of the perfectly straight asparagus, I heard the rattle! Looking down, where I was about to step, was a coiled anaconda-sized rattler! Taking the advised large step backward, I fell over the log blocking access to this off-limits area and I went flying. My glasses went flying as well and Chris and the dogs set off running. By the extreme grace of God, however, the snake didn't strike.

Sometimes God protects stupid. Sometimes He lets stupid take its course. I'm not sure why I'm including this in our book of songwriting. I guess it's to let you know that none of us are perfect, so our song may be off-key, but in Romans 8 we find that there is hope for the Spiritual Outlaw. P.S., Please don't let the Park Ranger read this!

Discovery Dialog with your Composer: Who did God come into the world to save? 1 Timothy 1:15.

Prayer: Lord, I love it that you love sinners. Thank You that You protect stupid!

Selah: The Lord is protecting me today, even from myself.

_____

_____

_____

_____

_____

_____

_____

_____

_____

_____

_____

_____

_____

Impossible to I'm Possible

I can do all things through Christ Who strengthens me.
Philippians 4:13.

I've heard it said among Christians, "God will never give you more than you can handle!" Who thought that up? I've actually found that the **opposite** is true: God gives me more than I can handle so that only He can do it and receive the glory!

There are so many examples of this "working against the odds" in the Bible. Gideon's army was cut from 22,000 to 300 so only God could get the glory. David removed all Saul's recommended armor before fighting the giant. The fiery furnace was made seven times hotter for Shadrack, Meschek, and Abednego. Jesus allowed Lazarus to remain dead for four days.

Think about it, if it's something I can handle in my own strengths and abilities who needs God? It is in my weakness that I am strong. It is when my defenses are gone that I find Him the Defender.

My "mission impossible" becomes my "mission possible;" my test becomes my testimony; the natural becomes supernatural. It has been said, if your dream doesn't scare you, it's too small. So dream dreams that, apart from Christ, could not be achieved. Sing songs that, apart from Christ, could not be sung!!

Though our family is musical, none of us can sing. Our common family joke is that the only Singer in our family was the sewing machine! **But God** (I love the "but God's" in the Bible!) has put a *new song* in my mouth. He's helped me find my voice in Josiah and the *impossible* has become *I'm possible* through Christ who sings over me and through me.

Your Composition

Discovery Dialog with your Composer: How does God rejoice over you? Zephaniah 3:13.

Prayer: Give me dreams and tasks today that can only be accomplished through you!

Selah: Today, with God's help I will move from the *impossible* to the *I'm possible.*

_____

_____

_____

_____

_____

_____

_____

_____

_____

_____

_____

_____

_____

_____

_____

_____

_____

_____

_____

_____

_____

_____

Valley of Dry Bones

The hand of the Lord was upon me and He brought me out by the Spirit and set me down in the middle of the valley, and it was full of bones.
Ezekiel 37

I realize this Ezekiel passage is about Israel becoming a nation during the end times. However, today it is for me! We at Heavenly Hope have been transported and set down in a valley of dry bones, and they are described as "very dry." Moms whose children have passed are often very dry; lacking hope.

I confess that continually sitting in a valley of dry bones can get quite depressing thinking about so many children, so many deaths, so many tragic stories.

Yet God's question comes to me as it did to Ezekiel, "can these bones live?" Like Ezekiel, I answer, "God, you know."

God leads Ezekiel to prophesy this over the dry bones: I will cause breath to enter you, that you may come to life! I will make sinews and flesh to cover you and put breath in you so that you may come alive and know that I am the Lord.

This is what keeps us sitting in the valley: watching God give breath to the moms who, like the sparrow, have hit the window and lost their child; watching them begin to move again and come to life!

What happens next? Verse 7, there's a noise and a rattling. The bones come together, bone-to-bone. Moms come alive, move and join our support groups and conferences, or just meet together bone-to-bone. Soon verse 10 comes alive: they stand and become a great army.

This is my big, hairy (literally) dream for moms: that they come alive and become a great army supporting other moms!

Discovery Dialog with your Composer: What happens when the graves are opened? Ezekiel 37:12-14.

Prayer: Put flesh on my dry bones, Lord. Make them become alive again.

Selah: Today my "dry bones" are coming alive and beginning to move!

_____
_____
_____
_____
_____
_____
_____
_____
_____
_____
_____
_____
_____
_____
_____
_____
_____
_____
_____

Three Moms, three Kids

For now we see in a mirror dimly, but then face to face. Now I know in part, but then I shall know fully.
1 Corinthians 13:12

Mary, Elizabeth, and Samson's mother were three pregnant moms who had experienced angelic appearances. Angels bore glorious prophecies to these women regarding their children and themselves as being favored and blessed mothers. Mary, your son will be called the "Son of the Most High" and will inherit the "Throne of David." Elizabeth, your son will be the Messiah's forerunner in the spirit and the power of Elijah. Samson's mother, your son would be set apart as a Nazarite to God.

So much joy, rejoicing anticipation, and celebration they must have experienced! Miracles and angelic appearances surrounding their births! My sarcastic, grieving-mother side wants to say to the angelic messengers, "Oh, and you forgot to mention, 'and Mary you'll see your son brutally crucified' and 'Elizabeth your 30-year-old son will be beheaded' and 'Samson's mom your son will commit suicide.' Why didn't you tell them <u>that</u>?" One son *gave up* His life, one son's life was *taken from* him, and one son *chose to take* his own life.

Did the angels have it wrong? Did the beautiful plans and prophecies go awry?

Because it is Biblically and historically recorded for us, we can see some of the "bigger picture" of their stories. Samson the "Nazarite Judge" was used to bringing about the death of thousands of Israel's enemies and acquire peace for Israel. John the Baptist's ministry needed to decrease so Jesus's could increase. Jesus needed to die so that I could experience salvation and have the hope of seeing my child again in heaven. Yet, God allowed each of these honored moms to suffer these horrible losses, including His own son's mom - she may have experienced the worst - losing 2 relatives, John the Baptist and Jesus.

Mary was warned in her prophecy, "a sword will pierce your own soul" (Luke 2:35). Did she remember this as Jesus's side was pierced by the centurion? Did Sampson's mom remember that the prophetic angel's name was "Wonderful" (Judges 13:18)? We certainly don't have the bigger picture, moms, but there is one and I'm looking forward to its revelation.

I was given a prophecy before Josiah was born by a preacher, not an angel. I'd have a boy and his name would be Josiah. Josiah, in the Bible, began his reign at eight in Israel and is known as the "boy king." What a strange way that played out!!

Your Composition

Discovery Dialog with your Composer: You may not have had prophecies regarding your child, but you certainly had dreams that were shattered by their death. Write them here. What does God say about these unfulfilled dreams? Isaiah 55:8,9.

Prayer: Lord, I don't understand "the big picture" but I desperately trust that there is one. As in Heaven, let it be on earth.

Selah: Today, I submit to God's will over my will.

_____
_____
_____
_____
_____

 *Paralyzed by the Pool*

When Jesus saw him lying there he learned he had been in this condition for a long time. He asked 'Do you wish to get well?'
John 5:6

The Pool of Bethesda still stands today outside the Lion Gate, with its five porches. Bethesda means "House of Mercy and Grace." The lame man surely needed both mercy and grace; he had been lying there for 38 years. He needed mercy, grace, and a Lion Gate!

Surrounded by these symbols of Himself, Jesus approaches the paralytic and asks what seems to be the obvious, "Do you wish to get well?" I can hear those around chuckling. Such a simple question, yet, so profound.

I don't mean to be insensitive, but I'm guessing that this man, after 38 years, had found some "pool pay-off" for not getting well. This man certainly had a reason not to join the labor force, as he received sympathy daily, had an entourage of people who ministered to him by taking him to the pool each day. He probably received alms from the fortunate and was feed through others. And, he probably received alms from the more fortunate. In addition to this, he also had a daily support group of people with whom he could commiserate, share and compare wounds. Surely after 38 years, his illness trumped most the others. He was in an uncomfortable place that had become comfortable in its familiarity.

Those in their first few years of grief need to lie by Bethesda, the pool of mercy and grace. They need to cry, wail, mourn, be ministered to, take time off of work (if one has that luxury). There is definitely a need for time to rest and to share your pain and your wounds.

However, I've met moms who are years down the road in their grief journey whose "muscles" have atrophied. They are paralyzed by the pool and can't move, much less have the strength to share a song in their sorrow.

If you're there, allow Jesus to whisper this question to you: "Do you wish to get well?" What are the pay-offs for not moving forward? Jesus commanded the man, "get up, pick up your pallet and walk!" We may be afraid that if we walk away we may lose our last link to our child - our grief. Jesus, however, lovingly let him keep his pallet with him as a memorial to his healing. I can picture it now: "See my pallet? I was paralyzed. Now I can move!"

Your Composition

Discovery Dialog with your Composer: Jot down any "pool-payoffs" that you may have been entertaining? Can you begin to release them today?

Prayer: Lord, I do wish to get well, heal me but let me keep my pallet as my testimony.

Selah: Today, I release any "payoffs " that are thwarting my healing

_____

_____

_____

_____

_____

_____

_____

_____

_____

_____

Our Heavenly Architect

Unless the Lord builds the house they labor in vain that build it.
Psalm 127:1

Anyone who's had the blessing or curse of building a house knows it takes tons of "blood, sweat, and tears." Decisions need to be made regarding materials, designs, colors, spacing, etc. Everything costs twice as much as expected and takes twice as long as anticipated. It is trying on one's relationships. Likewise, rebuilding one's life after a child has passed can have similar challenges.

I love the example of Abraham. He was looking for a *new* country and a *new* home. Hebrews states this *new* home has foundations whose *architect* and *builder* is God (Hebrews 11:10).

As I built a life after Josiah I knew I had to build it on the foundation of Christ and His Word. I had learned in Sunday school that, "the wise man built his house upon a rock ..." Matthew 7:24,25.

I am amazed to look back on these past 20 years and see that He has also been the *architect* - designing what I never could have designed, and *building* what I never could have built.

The buildings I have constructed with myself efforts, frenzied choices and wasted resources, have crumbled. Like the ruins of Pompeii, they lie in a pile of ashes. But Hallelujah! I have a "building of God," a house not made with hands, eternal in the heavens (2 Corinthians 5:1).

Our builder doesn't toil with "heavy equipment," His yoke is easy and His equipment is light. Better yet, it states in Hebrews 13:20 - He equips us in every good work to do His will.

Call on Him today to be your architect, builder, and supplier. When the next storm in life comes, and it will, your house will stand firm.

Discovery Dialog with your Composer: What are four guarantees made by the divine builder? 1 Peter 5:10.

Prayer: Lord, help me today to exchange my heavy equipment for your light load, and not labor in vain.

Selah: I will look to my Divine Architect for my plans for this day.

_____
_____
_____
_____
_____
_____
_____
_____
_____
_____
_____
_____
_____
_____
_____
_____

Who's My Neighbor?

You shall love the Lord your God with all your heart and with all your soul and with all your strength and with all your mind; and your neighbor as yourself.
Luke 10:27

The lawyer in Luke is struggling with the same questions that I struggle with daily: Am I loving the Lord with my all? Am I loving my neighbor as myself?

At my age, giving "my all" to anything is exhausting. I have to recover from getting dressed for exercise class! Spandex no longer just slips on!

My neighbors? In answer to the lawyer's question, Jesus relates the familiar story of The Good Samaritan. At that time, Samaritans were considered "half-breeds" and thus rejected by the Jews. The Samaritan is halfway on his journey when he passes a man described as being half dead. The nurse in me says, "come on, Jesus, one is either dead or not dead." However, the grieving-mom knows what it is like to be half-dead - to be robbed of their child beat up and lying half dead on the dusty road of life.

The half-breed meets the half-dead. (As the saying goes, "sometimes you're the bug; sometimes you're the windshield"). The other characters in our vignette are the religious Priest and Levite who only used their strength and mind to cross over to the other side.

Jesus clarifies that your neighbor is the hurting individual, that you, the imperfect person, encounters and helps along the path of life. He tells the lawyer "do this and you will find life."

It's in giving that we find living. It's in the giving to the hurting neighbor that we are pulled out of our half-dead state to live again.

Try it! Look for a hurting or "half-dead" person today to reach out to. Don't let your self-righteousness urge you to pass by. After all, he who gives his <u>all</u> to Jesus loses nothing.

Discovery Dialog with your Composer: What did Jesus tell the lawyer to do? Luke 10:37.

Prayer: Open my eyes to the "needy one" that cross my path today, help me to reach out with Your arms to them.

Selah: Rather than crossing to the "other side," I will help the hurting people I come into contact with along my journey today.

Consider the Birds of the Air

*Look at the birds of the air; they do not sow
or reap or store away in barns and yet your
Heavenly Father feeds them. Are you not
much more valuable than they?*
Matthew 6:26

Jesus instructs us to consider the birds of the air and the flowers of the field.

Geese flying in their "V" formation know exactly where they are going, rotating positions so as not to exhaust those in the lead. *Sea turtles* swim hundreds of nautical miles to return to the exact same beach they laid their eggs on two years prior. *Monarch butterflies* migrate thousands of miles to all arrive at the same location, in a different country, several generations later. How do they accomplish this? I get lost in the store parking lot!!

The flowers of the field? If you ever get a chance come to the Crested Butte Wildflower festival. There you will find, myriads of rainbow-colored flowers; not up to your ankle but up to your waist!! Arrayed in colorful bouquets, these flowers are strewn across the mountainsides. Jesus spoke of flowers when He said, "the women in Solomon's court were not as beautifully dressed as some of the field flowers."

Consider the flowers and as the old 70's saying went, "bloom where you are planted." In the same reference context of His taking care of your needs the condition is stated –seek first the Kingdom of God - and all these things will be added unto you. Everything!

Today I want you to relax about your song. Don't stress if you haven't found *your song. Your song* will find you! Maybe, like the

Monarch butterflies, it will be your next generation, or it may be someone *you inspire* that will carry *your song* to the next destination.

Discovery Dialog with your Composer: What else can we learn from the birds and flowers? Matthew 6:26-34.

Prayer: Open the eyes of my heart to notice the details of birds and flowers. Thank You that you so "much more" care for me!

Selah: I am aware of the signature of God in nature around me today.

_____

_____

_____

_____

_____

_____

_____

_____

_____

_____

_____

_____

_____

_____

_____

_____

_____

_____

_____

Sing to your Spring

See, I am doing a new thing! Now it springs up. Do you not perceive it?
Isaiah 43:19

A *new song*. A new thing. Not recycled or re-purposed, but new of a different kind!

Who doesn't like something new?

I've spent years rutting around thrift and antique stores, I used to love the musty, dusty smell that characterizes antique stores. Now, antique stores make me sneeze. I've realized that after spending the first half of life collecting things, I'm spending the second half getting rid of it all! Anyone need a nice silver-plated tray?

Psalm 40:3 states that God puts the *new song* in our mouth. This is not a song found on YouTube or in an antique hymnal. This is a *new song* - programmed into me by God.

Amy Dillard writes, "I've been my whole life a bell, but I never realized it until I was struck!"

God has programmed into us something very unique that comes out after we are "struck." Psalm 84:6 describes pilgrims who are passing through the Valley of Baca - the valley of weeping. As they pass this sad valley they <u>make</u> it a spring. In Numbers 21:17, the Israelites are in the desert and are told to sing to their desert so they can get water. A strange command, but it says the Israelites sang "Spring up O well!"

As you are passing through the Valley of Baca try singing to your desert. Watch for the "new thing" - "now it springs up, do you not perceive it? I will make a roadway in the wilderness and a river in the desert." Let go of the old whining, moaning, death dirge song and sing a *new song* - one that God places in your mouth.

Your Composition

Discovery Dialog with your Composer: What does Job say about the tree that is chopped down? Job 14:7.

Prayer: Thank You for Your promise that You will put a "new song" in my mouth.

Selah: I will sing to my desert and watch for its gurgle.

_____
_____
_____
_____
_____
_____
_____
_____
_____
_____
_____
_____
_____
_____
_____
_____
_____
_____
_____
_____

Four-Corner Friends

Since they could not get him to Jesus because of the crowd, they made an opening in the roof above Jesus by digging through it and then lowered the mat the man was lying on.
Mark 2:4

One of my wisest friends, Katherine Lee, has found a huge *new song* in her sorrow. Visit PureHopeFoundation.com to see and hear her song from sorrow. She has coined the term "Four-Corner Friends" after the four friends who each held a corner of the mat for the man who was let down through the roof to receive healing from Jesus.

The man on the mat was crippled and disabled to the point of not even able to entertain the hope of approaching Jesus. Remember those days? Maybe some of you are still in them? I can think back to some *four-corner friends* of mine who, when I was too weak to walk, crippled by grief, took me to Jesus.

These friends ironed burial clothes for Josiah, shopped for groceries, and pitched in to pay for house cleaners. One even filtered all incoming calls. Seemingly menial tasks, that were overwhelmingly huge for me at the time.

Consider the innovated friends in our story. During Jesus's time people frequently retired to their rooftops for the cool night air. Growing up, I assumed these rooftops had a built-in entrance with a ladder. However, reading this passage, it points out that besides carrying this man (who knows how far,) they find a way to drag him up to the roof and then dig a hole to let him through. These were consistent, persistent friends who strongly believed in Jesus's healing power.

Maybe you have never had "four-corner friends." Maybe you have had to drag your own paralyzed body to Jesus, or have had to wait for Jesus to find you.

Whatever was your scenario, the best way to "find-four corner" friends is to become one yourself. Start with a small, menial task like inviting a friend to hike or coffee. Start a small support group of grieving moms; there's a "how to" guide in <u>A Sparrow Falls</u>. God takes your little and makes lots!

The end result of the care from these "four corner friends" was the lame man being restored to physical and spiritual health. Look at your hand. You may hold someone's miracle mat in it! Look for a corner of someone's mat today and grab it!

Your Composition

Discovery Dialog with your Composer: Jot down any additional insights you gain from this story. Luke 5:19,20 and Mark 2:2-12.

Prayer: Help me be a four-corner friend to those who are paralyzed by life.

Selah: I will surround myself with "four-corner friends."

_____
_____
_____
_____
_____
_____
_____
_____
_____

The Invisible Made Visible

*Now faith is the assurance of things hoped for, the conviction of
things not seen.*
Hebrews 11:1

What are you <u>not</u> imagining? One hundred years ago no one could
even come close to imagining that people would make money
selling bags of dirt and bottles of water. Moreover, that people
would actually pay hundreds of dollars to go to a building to run,
sweat and experience physical pain and yet workout centers are
everywhere! The invisible has become visible; the imaginable a
reality.

God, who took the invisible and created worlds, can do the same in
our lives.

I never imagined writing a book. Half-way through the minutia of
it, I couldn't imagine finishing it either! However, God took the
invisible and created the visible, a physical book in my hand.

How about you? It doesn't have to be creating worlds or writing
books, but perhaps a local support group or a comfort basket
ministry.

According to our verse, it starts with faith, and then a heart twinge
of something "hoped for" and then an assurance of something *not
seen*. Combine this with God's invisible attributes, His eternal
power and His divine nature which are *clearly seen* (Romans 1:20)
and creation begins.

Opportunities appear, the invisible will become visible. The
impossible will become possible. Your child's passing will become
meaningful.

Pause today and ask the Holy Spirit, the revealer of truth, the Teacher, to show you something you might not be seeing.

Discovery Dialog with your Composer: What three things will the Holy Spirit do when He comes to you? John 16:13.

Prayer: Give me the faith to believe You for the invisible. Give me something to hope for and the assurance it could happen.

Selah: I am expectantly looking for the invisible and the unimaginable.

_____

_____

_____

_____

_____

_____

_____

_____

_____

_____

_____

_____

_____

_____

_____

_____

_____

_____

_____

_____

_____

My Mourning Star

I, Jesus … am the root and descendant of David,
the Bright Morning Star.
Revelation 22:16

From forming an astronomy club with my brother at age ten to attending a very nerdy astronomy club as an adult; I've always been a bit star-struck! Call us weird, but John and I frequently sleep outside. We enjoy this privilege because we live against a mountain and have a second-floor deck that provides protection from night predators (At least, I hope... so far).

I like sleeping outside because staring at the vastness of the night sky makes me acutely aware that there's a much bigger picture than my minuscule problems. John enjoys it because he likes to sleep next to me! My granddaughter, Alyssa, and I will sleep outside playing dot-to-dot with the stars and create star adventures. I got her a shirt that says "sleep under the stars."

Even though I grew up in Chicago and frequented the Planetarium, nothing prepared me for my first glimpse into a car-sized telescope in a dark campground in Wyoming. A gazillion stars appeared stars that I had been sleeping under every night but never knew existed. The Astronomy Club members explained that our galaxy, The Milky Way, has some 400 billion stars and there are 170 billion galaxies in the observable universe. Do the math, and you'll soon be star-struck too.

Hands down (or hands up in this case), my favorite is the One who describes Himself as the *Bright Morning Star*. He hovers over the skies of scripture, Old Testament to the New Testament.

Numbers 24:17, there shall come *A Star* out of Jacob, a Scepter shall rise out of Israel…" Luke 1:78,79, "*the Morning star* from on high shall visit those who sit in darkness and in the shadow of death …" That's why I affectionately refer to Him as my *"Mourning Star."*

Revelation 22:16, I Jesus… the *Bright Morning Star.*

What's this got to do with your song? Well, Job, who lost 10 children, his livestock, his friends and his health is shown a perspective of God's Sovereign Immensity! God shows Job the much bigger picture and even tells him of His chorus of singing stars (Job 38:7)! Listen to that chorus and begin to get your perspective and song back as Job did!!

Stop, watch it, be awestruck and inspired on Youtube - stars and whales singing to How Great is Our God, https://youtu.be/heixFeG-0n0

Your Composition

Discovery Dialog with your Composer: Why did the Morning Star come? 2 Peter 1:19, and Luke 1:79.

Prayer: Lord, You took Abram out and showed him the night sky. Tonight, as I go out and look at the starry host, remind me of Your bigger picture.

Selah: Nightly, I am reminded of Your bigger picture for my life.

_____
_____
_____
_____

The Great Grave Robbery

The tombs were opened and many bodies of the saints who had
fallen asleep were raised.
Matthew 27:52

Mary Magdalene had been robbed! She looked on in horror as the only man who had truly loved her was beaten and brutally crucified (John 19::25). Through teary eyes, she watched His limp body being removed from the cross and she followed the entourage to the tomb. Mark 15:47 says that Mary "sat opposite the grave" staring in disbelief.

Matthew 27:61 reveals that after two despairing nights she journeyed home to prepare the burial spices with the other women. Returning the next morning, while it was still dark, she received the final blow; the robbery of His body! The tomb was empty!! Falling to the ground weeping she cried, "they have taken Him and I don't know where!"

Josiah's death seemed to rob me of everything: his touch, his future, my future, my faith. Like Mary, I stared on in disbelief and horror as they wheeled his covered body out of the house, my mind screaming, No! No! This isn't happening!

Perhaps it was a robbery from Satan who comes to steal, kill, and destroy? Perhaps it was just the difficulty of life's circumstances? But Mary was soon to meet the Greatest Robber of all – Jesus!! He "robbed" first His own grave, in fact, He borrowed the tomb, knowing He'd only need it a couple of nights. And He's been robbing millions of graves since, including Josiah's. When I visit his grave, I know it is as empty as Jesus' tomb. The Great Grave Robber is the Resurrection and the Life!!

Mary is spoken of in Acts 1:14 and in Romans 16:6, where Paul says, "Greet Mary who has labored with me in this ministry." Which of the Marys, he didn't specify. I have no doubt that Mary Magdalene and the other Marys, and the disciples left singing that resurrection morning and found their *new song* after Jesus left this earth.

Your Composition

Discovery Dialog with your Composer: Can you handle an entire chapter? It will be worth it as it culminates in verses 55-57. Read and Sing! 1 Corinthians 15.

Prayer: Thank You for robbing Your own grave and that of my child's.

Selah: I am grateful that my child is more alive than I am.

_____

_____

_____

_____

_____

_____

_____

_____

_____

_____

_____

_____

_____

_____

_____

_____

Son-dial of Time

*Take heed, keep on the alert. You do not know when the
appointed time will come.*
Mark 13:33

Your "life story" takes a lifetime! You've perhaps heard the story of
the woman who approached the Carnegie Hall pianist and said,
"I'd give my life to play like you," to which the pianist replied, "I
did."

Beautiful things *don't* come easy "to those who wait." It comes to
those who have the courage to start. My bumbling attempts at a
song were messy and imperfect, and sometimes still are.

God lives outside of time but works in time. This morning I was
"camping" in Luke 13. Here I find a principle exemplified in 5
different stories.

- A fig tree that is not producing after 3 years and is about to be
  chopped down. The owner says let's give it **a year** and try
  fertilizing it (verses 6-9).

- The woman who has an illness and has been bent over for **18
  years** and she received an instant healing (verses 11-13).

- Next is the minuscule mustard seed that, **over decades**,
  becomes a large tree (verse 19).

- Anyone who has made bread can identify with the baker
  parable. Yeast rising in 3 pecks of flour takes **time** and
  observation (verse 21).

- Finally, Jesus closes with His time-line prophesy: I perform
  miracles today, tomorrow, and the **third day** I reach my goal
  (verse 32).

Maybe, like the fig tree, your roots need fertilizing for a year? Join a Bible Study. Feed on the fertilizer of the Word daily. Maybe like the woman, you've been bent over by life for 18 years? That's how long it took for me to "instantly" start Heavenly Hope and Healing. Your faith may be as tiny as a mustard seed but imagine it *could* be a tree someday! The baker's leaven began to rise in a dark, hidden place (we all have been there). Imagine having bread someday! Jesus chose to rise the third day, not the first. So many reasons, most of which remain a mystery.

Look to God's _Son-dial_ for your song. A life song takes a lifetime. Enjoy the mystery!

Your Composition

Discovery Dialog with your Composer: Is there anything regarding God's timing that you are anxious about today? What does Ecclesiastes 3 teach us about time?

Prayer: Lord, today I look to you for your appointed time to fulfill my desires.

Selah: While sitting in God's Waiting room I will remember there is an appointed time for everything.

Fanning the Ashes

A bruised reed He will not break; a smoldering wick He will not snuff out.
Isaiah 42:3

Staring at my son's ashes 20 years ago, I entertained the bizarre thought, "Hey, if I could just fan hard enough maybe these ashes will ignite!" Instead, the "smoke of the ashes" spread like grey fingers through our house and left me smoldering.

Today, I can say it is by God's fanning that I wasn't totally snuffed out.

I am aware that many moms reading this are too bruised and smoldering to think about composing a song.

Elijah was in this state as he sat on Mt. Carmel, depressed and described as having his head between his legs (in the fetal position?). The land was on its third year of famine which brought drought and death. King Ahab was blaming Elijah, "the troublemaker," for the famine. There was a bounty on his head. To save his life, Elijah blurted out a prophecy in Ahab's presence that there was a heavy shower coming. "I hear it," he said.

Yet nothing was happening! Too dejected to look up, Elijah assigned his servant to go look for the coming storm (keep a lookout for hope). Six times the servant reports the disappointing news, "there is nothing." On the seventh watch, a cloud the size of a man's fist appeared.

Now, in the great skies of things, "that ain't much." However, it ignited a smoldering spark of faith in Elijah. He yelled, "take cover, a heavy rain is coming!" The sky darkened and a strong wind came up. The floodgates of heaven opened!

Faith is the substance of things <u>not seen</u>. What are you not seeing that you'd like to see? Speak to your ashes; hear it coming. Let the wind of the Holy Spirit blow and <u>watch</u> for your "small cloud." When it does come, run with it!

Discovery Dialog with your Composer: In this story, at what point did Elijah feel the "hand of the LORD?" 1 Kings 18:41-46.

Prayer: Fan my dying embers and ignite a fire that others will come to watch burn!

Selah: Today, I will watch expectantly for my "small cloud," believing it will be followed by showers of blessings!

_____
_____
_____
_____
_____
_____
_____
_____
_____
_____
_____
_____
_____
_____
_____
_____
_____
_____

Abandoned Eggs

Can a woman forget her nursing child and have no compassion on the son of her womb? Even they may forget, but I will not forget you.
Isaiah 49:15

The Loggerhead Turtle Museum, located on the Florida coast, boasts the second largest sea turtle nursery in the world. March announces the turtles' yearly arrival. Slogging up the beach at night, the pregnant turtle will lay 100-125 eggs, meticulously covering them with sand, then ABANDON THEM.

The Museum curator explains that only one of these hundreds of eggs will survive the trip to and in the ocean. The others will be consumed by predators, tangled in plastics, or choked by ocean garbage.

What if the mommy turtle had stuck around to teach the baby turtles how to ward off predators and how to recognize and avoid ocean garbage? When I think of this, old feelings of guilt arise. Did I teach my son life skills and protect him enough? Did I somehow stomp on my egg? One would think that after 20 years of grief and growing I'd be beyond all this.

Interestingly enough, the mommy turtle travels a thousand miles in the deep, cold ocean and returns to the exact same beach two years later. Today, my thoughts return to the "beach" of Josiah's birth and life. Searching? Maybe. Remembering? Oh yes! But today, I return with the confidence that even if I had abandoned Josiah at any level, the Lord hadn't. He's never forsaken him or me!

Your Composition

Discovery Dialog with your Composer: What is God's promise to each of us? Hebrews 13:5.

Prayer: Thank You that You have never forsaken nor forgotten me or my child, and especially not in their moment of death.

Selah: I am never abandoned nor forsaken by my Heavenly Father.

Hemorrhaging

A woman who had had a hemorrhage for 12 years ... came up in the crowd behind Him and touched His cloak, for she thought, "If I just touch His garments, I will get well" ... Jesus, perceiving in Himself that the power proceeding from Him had gone forth, turned around in the crowd and said, "Who touched My garments?"
Mark 5:25-30

Recently, my close friend texted me that she had started bleeding from her uterus, which at the age of 65 is not good! It didn't take a village of doctors long to diagnose Stage 4 endometrial cancer!

Did our biblical lady suffer the same? Perhaps she had a miscarriage and there were no D&C's available? Whatever the cause, she had been bleeding for twelve years. This, in the Jewish culture, made her unclean and untouchable.

Aren't all of us who have lost children hemorrhaging from the uterus? That sacred space that first cradled our new little one. That womb/room where we first felt the quiver of life and laughed with our husbands as we watched our little one's heel slide across the belly wall and felt their kicks?

Some moms don earphones to their bellies and play <u>Baby Beethoven</u> hoping to create a budding musician. I recited multiplication tables to Josiah in utero and sure enough, he was a math whiz.

I've been hemorrhaging his loss for 20 years. Well, maybe no longer hemorrhaging, but trickling; always trickling his loss.

Pushing through the crowd to touch Jesus's garment was this woman's hope for healing! I can emphatically declare it has been mine too! Pushing through the crowded events of my busy schedule, I reach, stretching myself to just touch Jesus, even if it's just the hem of His garment. Somedays, when I do this I can feel His power "going forth" to give me hope and strength for the day.

While He was paying the price for our redemption at Calvary, the guards gambled for that same hemmed garment. Reach out and touch it today. It will bring the hope and healing that it brought to our biblical woman in Mark chapter 5.

Discovery Dialog with your Composer: What were Jesus' parting words to our woman? Mark 5:34.

Prayer: Lord, heal my hemorrhaging uterus. I believe only You can do this.

Selah: I will reach out in faith and touch at least the hem of Jesus's garment today.

_____
_____
_____
_____
_____
_____
_____
_____
_____
_____
_____
_____
_____
_____

Blessed-Overs

*The people ate and were satisfied. Afterward
the disciples picked up seven baskets full of
broken pieces that were "left over."*
Mark 8:8

John and I differ on leftovers. For example, I actually love Thanksgiving leftovers more than the dinner itself. Though often left on the restaurant table or forgotten in the refrigerator, I take restaurant leftovers home. As a child, John was forced to eat his uneaten dinner leftovers the next morning. This food was presented on a cold plate, with a cold fork, after being refrigerated all night.

There are two separate incidents where Jesus fed a hungry crowd from a few small fish and pieces of bread. Satisfying everyone as only He can do, He fed the entire multitude, and his disciples, with just a basketful of food and even had leftovers.

Two of the most unsung heroes of the Bible are the mom who packed that lunch and the boy who shared his few small pieces.

Like the lad, we willingly take our "broken pieces" to Jesus. He blesses them, and then miracles happen. The "ripple-effect" takes place. He takes our "not enough" and not only makes it "enough" but enough with "blessed overs!"

At Heavenly Hope and Healing we bring moms a "Comfort Basket" and soon this mom is contributing a heart-made item to our basket. Paintings, antique tea cups with garden mint tea, handcrafted boxes, quilts, bookmarks, and even dog tags with children's names on them. We have so much for these baskets that we now have "blessed-overs."

Maybe your coffee with a grieving mom will turn into a support group, hiking group, or outreach group, or you might be delivering baskets yourself. Miracles happen when we bring our broken pieces to Jesus!

Discovery Dialog with your Composer: What was the progression of distribution? How did the people feel? Matthew 15:35-38.

Prayer: Lord, bless my few broken pieces as I bring them to You. Multiply them like you did the fishes and bread - enough for those who need it, plus "blessed-overs!"

Selah: Today, I will encourage one other grieving mom.

_____
_____
_____
_____
_____
_____
_____
_____
_____
_____
_____
_____
_____
_____
_____
_____
_____
_____
_____
_____

Thief in the Night

Now a word was brought to me stealthily and my ear received a whisper of it ... disquieting thoughts from visions of the night when deep sleep falls on man.
Job 4:12-14

He came again last night, singing his whispering songs, filling my mind with should-have's, what-ifs, not-enoughness, fears about my future, John's future, my family's future, etc.

Stealthily circling my bedroom while stealing my sleep and my peace, he curled his dark hand around my brain with his fingers of half-lies and lies!

I switch on the night light of God's Word and cry out "O Lord! You who have been calling light out of darkness since creation. Expose these lies to the light of Your Word. Light dispels darkness."

In the morning, (when His compassions are always renewed) I write out the lies I heard in the night and allow God to shine the laser beam of His word and expose each.

Lie: John's got cancer. He's going to die. Truth: We're all going to die, but God knows the plans He has for me, to give me a future and a hope.

Lie: you're not making the right decisions. Truth: I will guide you in the paths you take with My eye upon you.

Lie: I am not enough for... Truth: You are complete in Me.

God said "let there be light" and again this morning there was light.

The thief is exposed and made powerless. Satan's song of lies fade and I am given a *new song* - color has appeared out of the blackness. Thank You for the truth of Your word that gives light!

Your Composition

Discovery Dialog with your Composer: What were the lies Satan told Job? What are the lies he is telling you? Write a verse of truth for each lie. Job 4:12-18.

Prayer: Lord, I can't fight this thief, but You can. Place your helmet of salvation over my mind especially at night. Let Your peace umpire and rule my heart.

Selah: Tonight, I will "cast down imaginations" and meditate in my bed about You.

_____
_____
_____
_____
_____
_____
_____
_____
_____
_____
_____
_____
_____
_____
_____
_____

Who's on First?

Now when He had risen early on the <u>first</u> day of the week He <u>first</u> appeared to Mary Magdalene, of whom He had cast out seven demons.
Mark 16:9.

Did Mary have "first dibs" on seeing Jesus in His resurrected body? As the pantomime of Jesus's last days unfolds, several women are sideline characters: Joanna, Jesus's mother, Mary, James's mother also called Mary, Salome, the wife of Cloas, the mother of Zebedee's son, and "other women."

However, Mary Magdalene is the only one noted as being in <u>all</u> scenes. She was the desperate, loving, sinful one. To whom much is forgiven, much is loved! After witnessing the horror of the crucifixion, Mary Magdalene watched as the body was taken down, given to Nicodemus, and laid in the grave. As the sky darkened into the night, she found herself sitting opposite the tomb heartbroken. We know what that one is like right moms?!

Leaving the tomb only to prepare spices, she returned early and found it empty. He <u>first</u> appeared to her and thus she is honored to be the <u>first</u> human to see Jesus alive! She was the <u>first</u> one to touch Him, the <u>first</u> one to notify the disciples, and the <u>first</u> one to get the ball of the Gospel rolling to the world; even as we hear it to today!

Did Jesus choose her? Or did she choose Jesus? Maybe both. What we do know is that her sinfulness didn't stop her from boldly approaching Jesus or Jesus reaching out to her. Previously, she had not one, but seven demons! There's hope for us mom and for our children!

She sought Him late at night and early in the morning. She pushed through tears and fears, grief and sorrow to look for Him. She believed His words about His future resurrection and watched expectantly.

Emulating her example, we too can have "first dibs" on seeing Jesus today and sharing our new song with others!

Discovery Dialog with your Composer: What was Mary's "new song" to the mourning and weeping ones? Mark 15:9-11.

Prayer: Today, I want "first dibs" on You. I watchfully seek You early in the morning and late at night. Reveal Yourself to me as you did Mary Magdalene.

Selah: I eagerly seek Jesus in the early morning and in the darkness of night.

_____
_____
_____
_____
_____
_____
_____
_____
_____
_____
_____
_____
_____
_____
_____

My Robin's Nest

*When my father and my mother forsake me
the Lord will take me up.*
Psalms 27:10

Today is Josiah's earthday-birthday. He would be thirty-six in earth years, and fifteen to eternal in heavenly years.

I've been watching my mama robin tending and defending her nest for over a month now. Today, as she broods, I'm brooding about Josiah and my mothering skills.

A robin almost always lays four eggs. I have four children. Hers have hatched and she hasn't lost one. I have lost one! The much too familiar regrets arise as I observe how aggressively she protects her nest, chasing off predators and calling for daddy robin when she needs backup! She is always alert, aware, and watchful.

John asked me to jot down Josiah memories to share with him today. Perhaps it's the robin, but all I can recall is six specific times that I didn't protect Josiah enough and bad things happened. I sob with the memories. My song is choked! John tries to console me with "the difficult things are what make us who we are" but I cry even harder with the regret of that one!

By this time, I am *so* attached to my robin and her hatchlings that I'd take on the wildest of cats to protect her. Why didn't I do the same for my own hatchling? Was I too trusting of acquaintances? Was I unaware of how mean and spiteful predators can be on gentle spirits?

I write Josiah a letter confessing my regrets and in doing so I become aware that he now has a full understanding of these events, and has forgiven me. God was there when I wasn't!

Watching mama robin forge and feed her babies, I realize I did a lot of things right too. I finish my morning with sharing a few good memories with John and he with me.

Guilt and regrets will stop the music. Go to God and find forgiveness for the guilt. Write a letter to your child and find forgiveness for your regrets. Sing with my mommy robin!

Within a week of writing the above, all the baby robins were killed in a hail storm. I am unbelievably heartbroken having watched them daily for two months. I guess even the greatest of mamas can lose all in the storms of life. I cry for her and all the mama's out there that have lost their hatchlings.

Your Composition

Discovery Dialog with your Composer: Who is the last enemy that will be destroyed? I Corinthians 15:25,26.

Prayer: Father, maybe our children died because of the storms of life or maybe The Predator Thief snatched them from us. Either way, thank You that You grabbed them up and they are safe in Your Wings today.

Selah: While I have breath, I will praise the Lord.

_____

_____

_____

_____

_____

_____

_____

 *A Gift from the Sea*

As a result we are no longer children tossed here and there by waves.
Ephesians 4:14

I pick up the sea glass, mesmerized by its frosted, opaque colors as it catches the morning's sand-sun. Like the surrounding, baited fish, I'm hooked! I love sea glass festivals, collecting at the break of dawn, and crafting amateur sea glass jewelry to display to my usually <u>un</u>impressed friends!

Europeans regard sea glass as trash. In their minds, it's the "garbage" they threw into the sea that should be left there. To me, each piece is a treasure like my fellow grieving moms.

Shards of a once brilliantly colored object are now weathered and broken, pitched onto our Heavenly Hope sands. As I stare at the treasures in my hand, I muse about their history: a piece of a ship's guiding lantern? A shattered serving plate from the galley? An ancient bottle tossed carelessly overboard? Someone's trash, my treasure.

Unique shapes of glass like unique moms with worn edges in myriads of color! Azure and cobalt blues, copper and reds, vivid greens, opaque with rainbow reflecting tones, and the rare lavender. All led to the beaches of Heavenly Hope, Umbrella Ministries, and groups like Compassionate Friends. Picked up to be admired by the treasure finders and beautifully repurposed.

Your Composition

Discovery Dialog with your Composer: How did Job compare his feelings to a piece of sea glass? Job 30:22.

Prayer: Thank you, Lord that as I was broken and tossed by violent waves of grief, You were forming me into something beautiful.

Selah: I will look for beauty as I hold my weathered, broken shard up to God's light.

_____
_____
_____
_____
_____
_____
_____
_____
_____
_____
_____
_____
_____
_____
_____
_____
_____
_____
_____
_____
_____
_____
_____

A Traveler's Tale

Jesus was traveling with them, but their eyes were prevented from seeing Him.
Luke 24:15,16

Two travelers were traversing seven miles of dusty road from Jerusalem to Emmaus. They were sad travelers, despairing at the loss of their beloved Master and Teacher. Yet, unbeknownst to them, He was journeying right next to them!

Were their eyes too swollen from grief to recognize Him? I know there were times when mine were too blurred with tears to recognize Him! He *was* marred beyond description, as Isaiah said He would be, and probably unfamiliar and unrecognizable.

When Jesus questioned them about their conversation they reply, "are you not aware of the event of these past few days?" In retrospect, I find this quite comical: Jesus who was brutally crucified not aware? Yet, He's kind in His response as He explains the Scriptures spoken over centuries that all point to Him.

We too moms, in our despair, on the dusty road of grief, will discover glimmers of hope coming from the Scriptures.

Courted by His words, the travelers take the vital next step: inviting Him into their home. Jesus was not going to intrude without an *invitation*. He was most likely headed for Galilee, but upon *invitation*, He entered their home, broke bread with them, and their grief-swollen eyes were opened to see Jesus! *Invite* Him in today to explain and give some sense to past events as you fellowship together.

Your Composition

Discovery Dialog with your Composer: What is Jesus waiting to do as He travels by the door of your heart-home? Revelation 3:20.

Prayer: Open the eyes of my heart Lord to behold You.

Selah: Today, I will practice the awareness of Jesus's presence as I travel my dusty journey.

_____
_____
_____
_____
_____
_____
_____
_____
_____
_____
_____
_____
_____
_____
_____
_____
_____
_____
_____
_____
_____
_____
_____
_____

God Uses Cracked Pots

But we have this treasure in jars of clay to show the surpassing power
is from God and not from us.
2 Corinthians 4:7

There we were three crackpots, mothers of loss, attempting to assemble six comfort baskets. This should be a simple task, right? But because of our brokenness, we were struggling. "Oops, two picture frames in this one…oh, oh no book in this one. Hey, where did our ribbon disappear to?"

Soon we were rolling on the floor laughing at how inept our attempts were for such a simple task!! Imperfection and vulnerability, by the way, can be a lot more fun.

My Tuscan patio and gardens are strewn with pots. With time, many have been cracked by the cold winter elements, trampled by wildlife, or knocked to their demise by the gusty mountain winds. Loving their patterns and vibrant colors, I've repurposed many of them.

As grieving moms, we have been cracked, shattered, and have had our feet of clay trampled by others and the cold elements of loss. We're all in this "Cracked Pot Club" together! But these cracks provide an opportunity for God's *glory glow* to shine through.

The "treasure" that's in the pots is described in the verse above: light shining in our hearts, the face of Christ, the image of God's glory, the light of knowledge. Quite the *glory glow* to entrust to an earthly vessel.

It's the <u>cracked</u> pot that best displays the light inside. The perfectly intact vase, grandly displayed on its pedestal, brings glory only to itself.

Our "cracks" can be filled with alcohol, drugs, shopping, or in my case, busyness. Or they can be left gaping for the world to peek in and see the face of Christ! He's in our brokenness.

Discovery Dialog with your Composer: What does God say to those who question how He has created their clay pot? Isaiah 45:9.

Prayer: Lord, shine your "glory glow" through the gaping cracks of my clay jar.

Selah: This little light of mine. I'm going to let it shine.

_____
_____
_____
_____
_____
_____
_____
_____
_____
_____
_____
_____
_____
_____
_____
_____
_____
_____

Biblical Bad Girls

*By faith the prostitute Rahab, because she
welcomed the spies, was not killed with
those who were disobedient.*
Hebrews 11:31

God is a God who specializes in redemption. He is no respecter of persons when it comes to an individual's past or even present state of sinfulness.

Rahab ran a house of ill repute in the red light district of Jericho. Yet, she was chosen to be David's great-grandmother and thus in the lineage of Christ. She, along with Sarah, and Rachel did their share of deceiving and lying but are mentioned in the Hebrews 11 **Hall of Faith**.

Jesus said He came into the world not for the righteous but for the sinner. He was, in fact, criticized for hanging with sinners (including a woman who was a prostitute and one who had been demonized).

You may imagine yourself too much of a sinner to deserve a song. Or worse yet, that your child was too "bad" to have their song sung. Not true. The Bible is full of sinners whose song is sung! The Apostle Paul called himself the "Chief of Sinners!"

Actually, moms, it was the Pharisee's *self-righteous* song that continually hurt Jesus's ears. He calls them whitewashed tombs, appearing clean and pure on the outside, but dead inside.

So, having seen the demonized and the deceitful, the harlots and the murderers blessed can you see there are no excuses for no song. The "Bad Girl Choir" went on to be blessed. Let us join their choir with our new song!

Your Composition

Discovery Dialog with your Composer: Who is Jesus kind to?
Read more about Rahab in Joshua 6:17, 6:25 and Psalm 87:4. I love
that bad girl. She had moxie! Luke 6:35,36.

Prayer: Thank You, Lord, for redeeming this sinner's life from
destruction and surrounding me with songs of deliverance!

Selah: Despite my past or present state of sinfulness, I will sing my
song.

_____

_____

_____

_____

_____

_____

_____

_____

_____

_____

_____

_____

_____

_____

_____

_____

_____

_____

_____

_____

_____

_____

Measuring Cups

God has allotted to each a measure of faith.
Romans 12:3

My husband tells me God has allotted me *big* measuring cups. I have *big* dreams, *big* goals/aspirations, and I hold them out to God who fills them and gives me more. John says his measuring cups are more like tablespoons or teaspoons.

Yet, when I think about cookies (and who does not want to think about cookies!), it may take four cups of flour, a half-cup of butter and sugar, but without the teaspoon of baking soda and the quarter teaspoon of salt, it would be nothing. John's smaller measure is essential for the success of the cookies.

Each person is allotted by God a "measure of faith." History is full of "big faith-ers" and "little faith-ers". "Big faith-ers," like Hudson Taylor who open the interior of China to the gospel, and "little faith-ers" like the elderly woman who opened the doors of her house for Hudson to teach the Word.

Will Rogers said, "We can't all be heroes because someone needs to sit on the curb and clap while they go by."

Maybe you're the clapper who encourages others to do their heroic acts! I have many clappers in my life and couldn't move forward in God's calling without them.

So know, moms, whether you have big cups or little cups (don't take that wrong!); whether you're a "big faith-er" or a "little faith-er;" a parade hero or curb clapper - you're not more or less valuable to God or His Kingdom. Seek what He has allotted you!

Your Composition

Discovery Dialog with your Composer: How can we get bigger measuring cups? Mark 4:24.

Prayer: Lord, use my measure of faith to enhance the recipe of Your kingdom.

Selah: Today, I will exercise my measure of faith.

_____
_____
_____
_____
_____
_____
_____
_____
_____
_____
_____
_____
_____
_____
_____
_____
_____
_____
_____
_____
_____
_____
_____
_____

So What in Heaven are They Doing?

The sparrow has found a nesting place; even the courts of the Lord.
Psalm 84:3

From the time he was little, Josiah knew how to make himself comfortable. His Third-grade teacher related how, during reading time, he would get on the floor, encircle himself with a blanket and read his book. We called it "nesting." Even as a 15-year-old, he would situate a sleeping bag around the heating vent, climb in the center, and play video games.

Now, "my sparrow" has found a nesting place in the courts of the Lord.

Josiah also hated being bored. He had my knack for mixing up words and said to me once, "Mama, I'm boring!" I knew he meant bored.

So what is going on in heaven? There are several times in the Bible where the heavenly curtain is rolled back and we get glimpses of activities that are taking place.

In 1 Kings 22:19-22, Micaiah has a heavenly vision of the Lord on the throne. The host of heaven is gathered around the Lord. He is entertaining a discussion about a situation that is about to happen on Earth regarding Ahab the king. As you read it, you find that God is actually getting the opinion of the heavenly host. He's seen weighing each opinion and then giving the command to go and do it.

Jacob (Israel), Daniel, the apostle John, and others, were given "fall on your face" visions of God on the throne, planning activity on Earth. I challenge you to feast on the colors and descriptions in these passages: Isaiah 6, Ezekiel 1&2, Daniel 7, 8, 9 and almost all of Revelation.

My dreams of Josiah are few and far between, however, shortly after he died he appeared to me explaining that he had come to me via "The Valley of the Four Lambs." Dream books explain that a valley is a transition; the number four represents elements of the earth, and the lamb would be God or Heaven; so Josiah was transitioning from heaven to Earth. I asked him what he did in heaven all day. Smiling, he replied, "God has an itinerary for me!"

Perhaps that was a significant dream, or perhaps I just had too much to eat the night before, but I like the idea that maybe our kids are co-operating with God to make things happen on Earth. Anyway, I like the idea and it makes me feel closer to God and to Josiah.

Discovery Dialog with your Composer: Since we are surrounded by a cloud of witnesses, how should I, then, live? Hebrews 12:1.

Prayer: As <u>in heaven</u> let it be on Earth today.

Selah: I will see your heavenly plan over my earthly one, today.

_____

_____

_____

_____

_____

_____

_____

_____

My Garden of Weedin'

… other seed fell among the thorns and the thorns sprang up with it and choked it.
Luke 8:7

As an avid gardener, I entertain a love/hate relationship with weeds. I love to eat them! I eat purslane in salads, I drink mullein tea, and I put organic dandelion greens in my smoothies. (Check it out: EatTheWeeds.com. Weeds labeled as "noxious" feels like unsolicited bullying to me!)

However, when they begin wrapping their skinny little green vines around my vibrant flowers with the malicious intent to choke, I do rise! I still don't want to poison them though, only feed them to myself or to my compost worms.

The sower's story in the Gospels shows its significance in that it is repeated in 3 encounters: in Matthew 13, Mark 4, and Luke 8. The gardener's seeds encounter one of six fates: snatched by the birds of the air, trampled underfoot, soil too hard or rocky to take root, scorched by the sun, choked by thorns and weed, or, it goes deep into the well-watered soil and yields a hundredfold crop!

Jesus pulled His disciples aside and warned them that some of these "Seed Snatchers" and "Song Stompers" are affliction, the evil one, persecution, worries, riches, pleasures of this life, mixing crops with woods, etc. Conversely, the seed that produces fruit has the soil of an honest and good heart, that bears fruit with perseverance (Luke 8:15).

Even today, I am aware of the "Song Snatchers" and "Seed Stompers," sending out their creeping little green vines to choke. But I am fertilizing and watering my seed in the Word and persevering.

In Matthew 13, "The Sower Parable," is followed by "The Mustard Seed Parable." The smallest of all seeds becomes larger than all the garden plants and becomes a tree that the "birds of the air come and nest in its branches."

I don't want to just be a big tree fruit-bearer. I want my branches to shelter and provide shade for moms as they nest in the branches.

Discovery Dialog with your Composer: How big does your seed need to be? Matthew 13:31, 32.

Prayer: Lord, protect my song from the evil one, and from others who want to snatch or stomp on it.

_____

_____

_____

_____

_____

_____

_____

_____

_____

_____

_____

_____

_____

_____

_____

Your Spiritual DNA

For we are God's handiwork, created in Christ Jesus to do good works, which God prepared in advance for us to do.
Ephesians 2:10

Did you know your spiritual DNA was designed and coded for you before you were even born? The Bible teaches that you were called before the foundation of the world (Ephesians 1:4). That excites me - that before I was good or bad, God created a song for my life!

Paul, when he was Saul, was bad. He persecuted Christians and gave consent to Steven's martyrdom. However, in Galatians 1:5, he states he was separated for God <u>from his mother's womb</u>. If I haven't "earned" my calling, I can't "un-earn" it either.

Here are some clues for discovering your God-given coding!

What did you want to be when you were a little girl? Some of my teacher friends would line up their dolls and teach them. Not me, I had a toy doctor's bag and said, "When I grow up I'm going to be a missionary nurse."

What were your favorite books? I loved *Heidi, Rainbow Garden,* and horse books. I live in the mountains, ride horses, and a garden.

What movies did you like (mine was The Secret Garden)? What songs did you like (of course, "His Eye is on The Sparrow!")? What makes you cry (I'm sad about sex trafficking, but *I* cry when I hear someone has lost a child)? You get the gist. Your "why" will make you cry.

Maybe your song has been muffled or stamped out by the hardness of this world. This is your time to get back in touch with your voice, The Composer, and your song.

Your Composition

Discovery Dialog with your Composer: When did God compose your song? Ephesians 1:4, and Jeremiah 1:5.

Prayer: Holy Spirit, revealer of all truth, You desire truth in my innermost being. Help me explore my purpose - for which God has created me.

Selah: I believe I am not here to just live life but to co-create a life with God.

_____

_____

_____

_____

_____

_____

_____

_____

_____

_____

_____

_____

_____

_____

_____

_____

_____

_____

_____

_____

_____

_____

Preview from

A Sparrow Flies

A Song That Outlives You

Even when you are old I will take care of you. Even when your hair turns gray I'll support you.
Isaiah 46:4

It's Your 80th Birthday!

Film writers always write their storylines beginning with the end. This approach helps them create their hero, villains, twists and turns.

Today, I want to throw out a fun challenge that has helped me live life more intentionally; keeping my priorities in line with my values.

Ready? Plan your 80th Birthday! Draw a square on a piece of paper with 6-8 circles (representing chairs) around it. By each "chair," write the name of the person you would like to have sitting there. You might even include your child or someone else who has passed.

Okay, did you do it?

On a separate piece of paper list your "core values." These are values that are unique to you - there are over 100 possibilities. Just google it. (For example, Family, Integrity, Fun, Work Ethic, Eating Healthy, God's Word, Fitness.)

Put a check by your top five. Yours will be different from mine.

Now, go back to the page and in the bubble next to each person, write what you would <u>like</u> them to be saying to you (not what they will be saying, but what you would like them to be saying).

Notice how everything you had on your "core values" list correlates with the bubble words.

This is how you can discover your Spiritual DNA! As you practice your part in life's play, make sure your decisions, activities, and daily choices, are all in alignment with your core values. Stay in character!

God knows the end from the beginning. The Alpha and Omega is your film writer. Life will take twists and turns, tragedies, mysteries, and surprises. There will be heroes and villains. When you live life with the end in view and stay in character, you <u>will</u> leave a legacy!

A Sparrow Sings
For Fathers

John Shelhamer

Contents

God, why did You do this?

Jesus made a scourge of cords, and drove them all out of the temple, with the sheep and the oxen; and He poured out the coins of the money changers and overturned their tables ... and the Jews then said to Him ... "What is Your authority for doing these things?"
John 2:15-17

In the Chronicles of Narnia Lucy is about to meet Aslan for the first time. She asks Mr. Beaver if he is safe. "Safe," said Mr. Beaver, "don't you hear what Mrs. Beaver tells you? Who said anything about safe? 'Course he isn't safe. But he's good. He's the King, I tell you."

The Jewish leaders were afraid of Jesus. He was good, but they knew He wasn't safe. They were afraid of Him.

The day after Jesus cleared the temple, they asked Him by what authority He did these things. He answered them with a question: The Baptism of John, was it from God or from man? (Luke 20:4)

Instead of facing the evidence and concluding rightly that it was from God, they rationalized the posture of their answer, like a chess game, and declared they didn't know. They were stuck on having things their way, and they refused to acknowledge the truth, so Jesus refused to answer their question.

This may be true of some of our questions as well, especially: "Why did You do this?" "Why did You take my child (or my loved one)?" He may be answering your question with a question of His own: "Did you commit your child to Me?" "If I were to have asked you the day before his/her death 'do you trust Me with your child's life?' Would you have said, 'Yes'?"

If we are unwilling to recognize and humbly accept the truth of God's part and God's authority in what happened, He may not show us the answer either. "'Course he isn't safe. But he's good. He's the King, I tell you."

The Apostle Paul said, "Should we sin that grace may abound? … Don't be stupid!" Similarly, "Would God do evil that good may come? … Don't be stupid!"

God is not tempted by evil and He does not test anyone with evil. In him is no darkness, no not any. Psalm 94:20, *"Can a throne of destruction be allied with You, one which devises mischief by decree?"* The answer is obvious.

Good and Evil 101: If it has to do with stealing, killing or destroying, where does it come from? Yes, it comes from the devil. If it has to do with life, and particularly abundant life, where does it come from? It comes from the Lord.

Okay, we have to push "pause" here for a moment. Does God ever "take" a life? Does He ever cause death? The short answer is, "Yes." But the longer answer is, "In judgment." God has, in the Scriptures, put individuals to death, but it is almost always in judgment.

Is my loved one's death a judgment from God then? No. How do I know that? 2 Corinthians 5:19 *In Christ, God was reconciling the world to Himself, not counting their trespasses against them. God is not judging you or your loved one.* He will judge one day, but not today.

Push "play" again: There is sowing and reaping. We do reap what we sow, and unfortunately, sometimes we reap what others have sown. God didn't take your son's life, it was a drunk driver who took it. God didn't take your daughter, leukemia did. God didn't take your wife, diabetes did. Sometimes God steps in and stops these terrible things. Sometimes He doesn't.

God didn't stop my son from taking his own life. But He did step in and save my daughter. She was ejected through the rear window of a Ford Explorer when it hit a patch of ice at 70 mph. Believe me, I have wondered and asked Him why. I don't have an answer. What I really want when I ask (more than an answer), is: I want the truth about Who He is and How He works.

I have to confess, there are times, maybe more frequently than I'd like, when I fear calamity. I fear tragedy striking my family, hurting my heart, upsetting my world again.

I'm sure it is a reaction to past tragedy or tragedies. It's a defense mechanism to keep me from being surprised by tragedy again. To live with this is to live with fear. I will not do that. God has not given me a spirit of fear, but of sound judgment.

Perfect love casts out fear. His love casts out fear. Fear is trusting in evil, trusting in punishment. The only remedy is to trust in His control over our chid's life. Trust in His wisdom, kindness, and His goodness. Is He safe? No, but He is good.

On Your Own:

2 Corinthians 1:9 Although you may really want to know "why" and "why now" or "why this way," are you willing to express your trust in God? Write out a statement of trust for today.

Prayer:

God, I know you are always saying, in one way or another, "Trust Me." That is hard sometimes. I did trust You, and see what happened? Okay, I do bow my heart and affirm that I trust You. Cast out my fear.

Affirmation:

God is my refuge. I am looking for good today. Psalm 16:1,2

Christian Karma

Without faith it is impossible to please Him, for he who comes to God must believe that He is and that He is a rewarder of those who seek Him.
Hebrews 11:6

Do I believe that God is a rewarder of those who seek Him?

I do believe it, in that I have come to Him every day for these many years, yet not for a reward, but because He is my salvation. He is my life. He is my breath, my strength, my ability to believe that life is worth facing every day. The result is that He has blessed. If all the blessed in the world were lined up, I'd be near the front of the line.

If it were not for the touch or contact or guidance He gives me each day I would soon conclude that my only purpose here on earth is to enjoy what I can while I can. But a rewarder? Hmm. I'm not sure I should come to Him because I want to be rewarded or paid for it. I come because I don't think I can exist without Him. The reward is a bonus.

In Matthew 10:10 Jesus said that the laborer is worthy of his pay. Is this different from Karma? Or is it different from a "God-ordained" Karma?

I'd say, "Yes, it is different." Karma is good payment for good deeds; bad payment for bad deeds. Reward, on the other hand, in God's way of working, has the element of reward for trusting Him in suffering, for trusting Him for vengeance, or even trusting Him for good to come my way.

Christian Legalism is probably more like Karma, "Christian Karma." When I am stuck in legalism I'm always afraid that my good isn't good enough and my bad is going to make God treat me badly, or at best, ignore me. There's this reoccurring thought in the back of my mind: "He will stop blessing me if I don't …" or "He won't be good to me if I keep doing tis, or thinking that."

God rewards as a Father, not as a judge. Do His rewards demand obedience? Maybe I'd be better off saying He <u>desires</u> obedience; what <u>demands</u> obedience is a life of faith. Either way, the reward far exceeds what is deserved. Divine generosity, rather than human merit.

This is certainly different from Karma. Karma is merely tit for tat. God's reward, on the other hand, is a semi-load for a pathetic handful. We bring a meager offering (out of what He gave us in the first place) and He gives to us beyond what we ask or think. When we behave badly, there may be bad consequences, but God will still treat us favorably because of His Great Love for us. He is <u>for</u> us, not against us.

So, Lord, I don't come to You, and I don't think I <u>should</u> come to You, because I want to be rewarded or "paid" for it. I come because I cannot exist without it, without You, without a touch, a confirmation, an encouragement, an insight or counseling from You.

I certainly haven't earned enough credits to deserve something from Him. I come to the Lord, not as an employee or a worker, but as a beggar, maybe even as an addict. Yes, I am addicted to Him!

So, the thought of *he who comes to Him must believe that He is … a rewarder of those who seek Him* is almost a trick question. I guess I'd say I come believing <u>that</u> He rewards, but not because He rewards. The only reward I'm looking for is that He respond to me and help me; let me know He's here, and answer my prayers. Does that make sense?

On Your Own

Isaiah 55:6 How often do you seek the Lord? When you do seek Him, what exactly are you seeking? Write out a statement that affirms your belief that He rewards your seeking.

Prayer:

Lord, I know I often seek Your hand, asking you to take it out of Your pocket and do something for me. Right now, I want to seek Your face, to see You, to know You are near, to comprehend that You are for me.

Affirmation:

Use the statement you created under "On Your Own" as your affirmation for today.

Regrets and Pushing Forward

*I press on toward the goal for the prize of the upward call of God in
Christ Jesus.*
Philippians 3:14

This Scripture is using the metaphor of a foot race to teach us
about pressing forward and not falling back. I'm a runner. I wasn't
always one, but I get the metaphor.

Near our house is a "feature" - The Manitou Incline. Google it
some time. It is an old cog railway. It goes up about 2100 feet in a
little over a mile. I did it for the first time not too long after Josiah
died. In fact, when I did it I thought I would die.

Then I started doing it more often thinking, "If I really push it I
might have a heart attack and join him." After a few months my
thinking changed to: "Great, if I had a heart attack now I'd
probably survive. That would be even worse!" Now I'm an addict.
My wife says that if I don't run for two or three days I run in my
sleep.

When I began my grief journey, it was like when I started running:
tough. Run a little, walk a lot, wonder why I'm doing this. But
more and more it became a way of life, "It's what I do." I've got to
do it, I'm addicted. It's my mood drug. In fact I've found that
exercise can positively affect my mood and my day better than any
drug. Any more I feel I can't <u>not</u> do it. I do not want to be *of those
who shrink back.* (Hebrews 10:39)

As a runner, I often try to calculate, how long will this run take?
Sometimes it's a long run, like the Grand Canyon. I have to tell
myself, "Don't even think about it at all, just know it will be a long
time!"

It is often that way with grief. We wonder, how long will this pain last? How long will I be sad? How many times will I think about what I should or shouldn't have done? In fact there's a lot of similarities between a grief journey and a race.

Sometimes it's all uphill. The pace is slower, and more tiring. Definitely more work. Persistence is the only thing that will get you to the top of a mountain Sometimes it boils down to telling yourself, "Just keep your feet moving." That's when I quote to myself Isaiah 40:31, *They will run and not get tired.*

Sometimes it's downhill. Much easier, more fun, but challenging just to keep your feet from tripping or mis-stepping. Then I'm quoting Psalm 91:12, *His angels … will bear you up in their hands, that you do to strike your foot against a stone.*

Sometimes it's on the beach. There I find myself breathing the sea level oxygen, feeling the warmth, running with my eyes closed and my arms outspread, feeling the freedom and exhilaration of all. There are days like this, too, when I feel like "this could go on forever."

It is the same with grief: Run a little, walk a little, wonder a lot. But the one constant is time with God in His word. This is my salvation: to read and pray and memorize.

My stretching exercise? Writing down, every day, things I'm thankful for. Then, asking God to meet me today. I tell Him I cannot make it through the day without Him helping and guiding me. I ask Him, "Please let me know You're here for me today."

So what does this have to do with regrets and pushing forward? I believe that Paul had plenty of regrets. He persecuted Christians. He pursued and imprisoned Christians. He approvingly held the coats of those who stoned righteous Stephen to death. Ananias, before he prayed with Paul for healing and salvation, exclaimed to God, *Lord, I have heard from many about this man, how much harm he did to Your saints at Jerusalem; and here he has authority from the chief priests to bind all who call on Your name!*

How did Paul live his Christian life? To tell us, he used the metaphor of running a race: *Forgetting what lies behind and reaching forward to what lies ahead, I press on toward the goal for the prize of the upward call of God in Christ Jesus.*

Forgetting, pressing, running, reaching. Leave the difficulties behind you. Put your regrets out of your mind, You have been forgiven. Forget that you could have done things differently and convince yourself that you did the best you could with what you knew. Reach forward to what lies ahead: healing, wholeness, renewed purpose, beauty for ashes, garments of praise. Keep pressing, keep running forward, running to grab what Christ Jesus has for you. Some days are uphill. Some days are downhill. Some days are like running on the beach. Don't think about the competitions you've lost, you'll never be able to win. Learn from them. Move forward. Keep running, running for the prize.

On Your Own:

Hebrews 12:1,2 What is the best way for you to run this race?

Prayer:

Lord, give me the persistence and the strength to keep going. Some days I find it difficult to walk through the day, but with your help every day, I know I can learn once again to run, jump, play, and sing!

Affirmation (here's two today):

I am constantly aware of God's presence helping me and lifting my countenance today. (Psalm 42:5,11, Psalm 3:3)

Because He has satisfied me with His lovingkindness this morning, I am singing for joy and gladness all day long. (Psalm 90:14, Psalm 143:8)

Don't You Care That We Are Perishing?

Jesus Himself was in the stern, asleep on the cushion; and they woke Him and said to Him, "Teacher do You not care that we are perishing?" And He got up and rebuked the wind and said to the sea, "Hush, be still." And the wind died down and it became perfectly calm. And He said to them, "Why are you afraid? Do you still have no faith?"
Mark 4:38-40

Jesus is the ruler of the wind and the waves. I find myself just like the disciples, who found themselves crying out about their circumstance. Yes, Jesus rebuked the wind and waves Then He rebuked them for their lack of faith. He addresses their soul, their faith, or lack of it.

Should I conclude that troubles are about our soul? Our faith? Are troubles all about trusting God? What was Jesus saying their expectation should have been in this situation? Should they have rebuked the wind and the waves themselves? Should their request of Jesus have been different?

Maybe they should have said something like, "Lord, You have the power, bring this storm under control!" But isn't that pretty much what they said when they shouted, "Lord save us!"

Maybe the expectation was that they should have said to one another, "The Lord is with us, we won't sink." Or, "He won't let us sink." We can think that, but we still need to shout "Lord, save us!"

Maybe the rebuke was because they said, "Don't You care?"

What would have been an appropriate expression of faith? In the conversation that followed, two more times he mentioned their lack of faith.

On the surface it seems that they did the right thing, the thing of faith: they asked Jesus to calm the storm. Was He expecting them to just ride it out and say, "God has a purpose for this storm. Let's just see what it is"?

I find a key to understanding Jesus' rebuke is in: "Why are you fearful?" Here they are, in the boat, with the Master, after the Master had said, "Let's get in the boat and go to the other side," and they were fearful. Calling on the Lord to calm the storm was the right thing to do, but being fearful wasn't. Their fear betrayed their lack of faith.

Sometimes in life we find that, in a sense, we have let Jesus fall asleep in the back of our boat. Then a storm comes. Life and tragedy takes us by surprise. This is the time to call to Jesus, "Save us, we're perishing!" It is not the time to think that God is not paying attention, or that He won't answer our prayers, or that He's trying to drown us. It is the time to have faith, not fear.

On Your Own:

Psalm 91:14,15 Jesus made it clear that, *in the world you shall have tribulation.* What do these verses say God has in store for you? Can you believe what He promises in verse 15?

Prayer:

Lord, I am calling upon You. Lift my feet out of this trouble. Rescue me from the terror. Fill me with Your faith, mine is inadequate.

Affirmation:

God is delivering me today, because He loves me.

A Sacrifice of Thanksgiving

*Enter His gates with thanksgiving and His courts with praise. Give
thanks to Him, bless His name. For the LORD is good; His
lovingkindness is everlasting and His faithfulness is to all
generations.*
Psalm 100:4,5

Today is Thanksgiving Day. What a great day! Much to be thankful
for. This house filled with the noise of family and the smells of
baking turkey, cooking vegetables, baking bread. Loved ones are
here, noise, happiness, games all fill the house.

Most, if not all, of our mothers taught us to be thankful, or at least
to say, "Thank you" when someone did something for us, or gave
us something. Being thankful is just plain good manners. That
thankfulness is a thankfulness that can be given and received
without surrendering self-sufficiency, arrogance, or our own will. It
is the acknowledgement of a kind act or a thoughtful gift.

On the other hand, there's thankfulness that must come out of
humility; a thankfulness that recognizes that you have been given
things that you do not deserve, gifts that you have not earned and
that, in reality, you are not capable of providing for yourself. This is
a thankfulness that comes with an acknowledgement of the
inadequacy and emptiness that can only be filled by a kind Creator
who is in and of Himself, all-sufficient, generous and loving. This is
thankfulness that, when offered to God, is true worship.

When my life is plagued by trouble, I find myself asking God,
pleading with Him to rescue me. A more fruitful response is to
praise Him and thank Him for what He is going to do, and what
He has done. How hard is it to be thankful <u>after</u> God has rescued
me? I wonder, how often God waits to hear my thanksgiving <u>before</u>
He rescues me? Give Him a sacrifice of thanksgiving, expressing
your confidence in what He <u>will</u> do because of your faith in Him
and because of His great love for you. God will rescue you. He will

redeem the death and trouble that has come your way. He is healing you. He has promised that!

Ps 50 - *Now consider this ... He who offers a sacrifice of thanksgiving honors Me.* And, *To him who orders his way aright I shall show the salvation of God.*

In the gospels Jesus often gave thanks to the Father. His thanksgiving was an expression of appreciation, an acknowledgement that, in His humanity, He was dependent upon the Father. Could we do any less?

Sometimes it is painful to think about my son. As I think about my son today and I stir up my heart to remember things for which I am thankful. This is a sacrifice of thanksgiving. I meditate on being thankful: For the memories of his voice, his silky hair, the little stubble growing on his chin, his almond eyes. For him on stilts, on a unicycle, with his juggling balls, his Pong chips, his Looney Toon drawings, his Adventures in Odyssey tapes, his Garfield everything, his lighting his farts on fire, his snowboarding the stairs, his overwhelming and never ending desire to be in heaven. For seeing him sitting in my office chair reading my Far Side calendars. For the way he would make his crepes float in syrup. For the way he would self-ration his Halloween candy, making it last for months. For his quick whit and the way he would constantly think outside the realm of "normal." For his sweet spirit, and how he was such a good child. For his love for the ocean and the beach; his love for his cat.

Thinking on these, and being thankful for these helps me think beyond and above the "defining moment" of his death. It's so hard to get beyond that, but there is so much good to be seen once I look beyond, and thank God for what I *do* have, what I *did* have, and what I *will* have. This is the kind of thankfulness that will put a song in your heart.

On Your Own:

Psalm 50:23 Spend some time writing out as many positive memories of your child you can recall.

Prayer:

Heavenly Father, Thank You for the pain in my heart that reminds me of how much I loved my child. Thank you for turning my attention to the good that was in him (or her), and the fun times we had together. Reduce my pain as I express my thanksgiving.

Affirmation:

Today I am replacing every terrorizing thought and every painful thought with thoughts of gratitude and good for the time we shared together on Earth.

Jehovah-Rophe, Jehovah my Healer

For I, I AM (the LORD), your healer.
Exodus 15:26

For several years I had suffered from sleep apnea. Sometimes my wife would shake me awake and say, "Wake up! You haven't breathed for a couple minutes!" Or I would bolt up in bed gasping for air.

I never thought to ask God for healing. One day I told my pastor about it just in a conversation. He exclaimed "We need to pray for your healing!" He grabbed an old saint (ancient actually, Albert was probably 90 at the time). He took me into his office, anointed my head with oil and prayed for my healing. As he was praying, God very clearly brought to mind some sins I needed to confess and repent of. I did. I have never had sleep apnea since that day.

So now I can, and do, say, "Thank You, Jehovah-Rophe, my healer for healing me and my family. Foremost, for healing us from Josiah's death, but also, for me, my sleep apnea, my shoulder, lung and ribs, my head, my feet, knees and hips so I could still run, and whatever else I have not thought of or not even been aware of!" (My ophthalmologist said, "Whoever did laser surgery on your detached retina did an excellent job." I told him "I've never had a detached retina." He went on, "Well, I'm just saying, It was repaired, and it was perfect.")

With His stripes you have been healed. 1 Peter 2:24 The prayer of faith will heal you. When you pray, ask, believing you have received, and it shall be unto you. Mark 11:24

I have come to realize that some healings are immediate, without medical intervention. In other cases God will use the hands of a skilled physician. He has miraculously healed my daughter's melanoma, my wife's Lyme's disease, my friend's stage-4 lymphoma.

Those healings happened quickly. The healing of grief is never quick. It is a long-term deal. There's no such thing as instantaneous grief recovery. It is miraculous however, because true healing from grief is a gift from God. It is a healing many never find. God's healing gives you life where once you only had existence. God's healing gives you life in exchange for your existence.

I have had some painful experiences in my life. Some have been physical and some emotional. But when my son died I learned that I never knew a human being could experience such pain!

Five years later, on the anniversary, I told a group of friends "I feel like I'm just beginning to come back to life." One woman's mouth dropped open. But then, her kids were two dogs. What does she know?

But now, I say, "Thank You, Thank You, Thank You, Father above all others for healing my soul, my wife, my family, my life." If we continue to seek His face, day after day, He will heal us with life in exchange for what we thought was life. Believe He is good; believe He has good for you; believe He has a miracle of joy and gladness for you; believe He will give you songs in the night, songs in the morning, songs in the day. John 10:10, He came to give life, not to take it.

On Your Own:
2 Corinthians 4:6 Even if you cannot feel it, what can you be sure is happening to and for you today?

Prayer:
Dear God, Give me greater strength, courage and joy each day. Progress seems so slow, but I trust that you are working to make me whole.

Affirmation:
Today I am continuously looking for things for which I can be grateful. These are signs that God is surrounding me with life.

Why One and Not Another?

Can you discover the depths of God? Can you discover the limits of the Almighty? They are high as the heavens, what can you do? Deeper than Sheol, what can you know?
Job 11:7,8

The day my son, Josiah, killed himself I was working with a client in a distant state. On my journey home, I was stranded in the Phoenix airport because my flight home was canceled. As I headed for a hotel shuttle I felt strongly that I should call home. I walked to a pay phone, put my hand on it, changed my mind, and walked away.

A short time later I had the same strong urging again. So I called. My wife told me that our son had killed himself. During my all-night journey home I questioned why God didn't give me the same urging to call hours earlier when Josiah was home alone.

A few weeks later we received a call from our daughter. She had been in an accident. She and two of her friends were coming back from snowboarding. They were traveling from Breckenridge on the freeway through the mountains at about 70 mph.

She was asleep in the back of the Explorer when they hit a patch of ice and spun around. Then they hit a dry patch and she was ejected through the back window. She landed in the median on all fours, looked up and saw the Explorer rolling toward her. She scrambled out of the way just before it rolled over the spot where she had landed. Barely a scratch.

One of my first thoughts was, "Why would You step in and spare her, Lord, and not step in and spare Josiah?"

This morning I was reading about Jesus and His disciples in the Upper Room. After Jesus announced that one of them would betray Him, they began discussing who it could be. Then they began asking Jesus, *Lord, is it I?*

Judas, so as not to appear to be the one, also said, *Lord, is it I?* Apparently he was sitting close enough to Jesus that the others didn't hear Jesus reply, *It is as you have said.* He apparently said it so quietly / discreetly, that even John, who was sitting right next to Him, didn't hear the reply and said to Jesus *Who is it?*

Jesus knew who Judas was, what he was going to do, what the result would be. He had eleven other strong men with Him. He could have easily prevented the betrayal with a word. If He had just said, "Judas is the one. We need to eject him from our group," the betrayal would have ended.

But He didn't. By not stopping the evil, sin's blindness and cruelty accomplished the greatest gift for mankind ever. As Dr. Paul Tripp put it, "At the cross of Christ, ultimate good and ultimate evil kissed."

I began thinking, "What other 'evils' did God or Jesus not stop?" Jesus didn't stop the death of His own father (which may be why his brothers did not believe in Him until after His resurrection). He didn't stop the death of Lazarus - which resulted in that amazing resurrection miracle, which in turn, resulted in fueling the Jewish leaders' plan to kill Him. God didn't stop Saul's pursuit and persecution of David, which resulted in much of the Book of Psalms, which has resulted in the strengthening and encouraging of millions, possibly billions, of saints. God didn't stop Eve's sin. Perhaps all He would have had to do was to speak to Eve and tell her, "The devil is going to tempt you. He is going to try to deceive you by saying, 'For God knows that in the day you eat from it your eyes will be opened, and you will be like God …'" But He didn't.

The Bible does say that right now the Holy Spirit is "restraining" evil. Which means that sometimes He steps in and stops it.

Sometimes He doesn't. As much as we would like to know why; as much as we would like to have the say, we don't know why He does do or doesn't do. This is where pure faith saves our sanity, when we say, "I trust You. I choose to believe You are good." What does He give us to hold on to? Ps 23:4 *Though I walk through the valley of the shadow of death, I will fear no evil; for You are with me.* He is with us.

I'm so busy asking Him questions, I seldom stop and hear Him ask me, "Will you trust Me? Do you believe I am with you?" If you need peace trust is the key. When we trust Him, His gift in return is to give us peace. Isaiah 26:3, *The steadfast of mind You will keep in perfect peace, because he trusts in You.* Trust in the Lord forever.

On Your Own:
Psalm 40:5 How can this verse help you answer the question God may be asking you: Do you trust Me? How is it possible to trust God when He does not stop evil?

Prayer:
I know the path to peace is trust. Help me to trust even when I don't understand.

Affirmation:
I have perfect peace today because my mind is focused on the Lord.

Encourage Yourself in the Lord

Why are you in despair, O my soul? And why have you become disturbed within me? Hope in God, for I shall again praise Him for the help of His presence.
Psalm 42:5

Some mornings I wake up and just feel all wrong. Today was a morning like that. I feel like I'm wrong, like my life is wrong, that everything could go badly. Maybe it's something I did, or watched, or dreamt. Maybe it's an evil spirit or a memory haunting me. Or maybe it's reality, as I realize how fragile life can be and how insufficient I am to make it work for me.

It's mornings like this, Lord that I especially need Your presence. Oh, yes, I need it every day, I know that. But it's days like today where it becomes my survival, my salvation. I guess I don't need it more today, but I sure feel it more.

Ps 22:4 *In You our fathers trusted. They trusted, and You delivered them.* I feel so grateful that I have a Bible that tells me of those who have gone before me with much less information about God and still walked by faith with the courage and faith to trust Him.

I am also thankful that Jesus experienced the isolation that some feel, when He said, *My God, My God, why have You forsaken Me?* Certainly the wolves and the lions had surrounded Him. Verse 19, *But You, O LORD, be not far off ... hasten to my assistance ... deliver my soul ... save me from the Lion's mouth ... I will tell of Your name to my brethren.*

Today I feel the wolves are still circling my family and nipping at us. More of the office phones went out. Nip. Trouble for my programmer with encryption keys. Nip. My wife's nasty and infected bug bite. Nip. Trouble with my van. Nip.

I've got to encourage myself in the Scriptures. This is what I found today:

> Ps. 27 *I would have despaired unless I had believed that I would see the goodness of the Lord in the land of the living.*

> Ps. 16 *I have no good besides You, Lord.*

> Ps. 22 *Be not far from me, for trouble is near.*

> Ps. 31 *I trust in You. I say, "You are my God. My times are in Your hand."*

> Ps. 34 *I sought the Lord and He answered me and delivered me from all my fears.*

> Ps. 62 *My soul waits in silence for God only. From him is my salvation. He only is my rock and my salvation, my stronghold. I shall not be greatly shaken.*

> Ps 73 *Whom have I in heaven but You? And besides You, I desire nothing in the earth. … As for me, the nearness of God is my Good. I have made the Lord God my refuge that I may tell of all Your works.*

Suddenly I see, in the midst of trouble, the blessings He has sent.

On Your Own:

Of the Scriptures listed above, which one do you most connect with, or which one means the most to you? Read that entire Psalm and make the Psalm's exclamations your own.

Prayer:

Maybe it seems that the wolves are still nipping, even dragging some off. So pray, "Lord, call off the wolves. Send them scurrying away so that You can bless us. As I ask for this, may You be glorified by the answer. We are insufficient, You are all sufficient."

Affirmation:

God is for me today, not against me.

Can you hear Me now?

Other sheep ... shall hear My voice ... and follow Me.
John 10:16

I remember the day I first thought: Does God actually speak to me? I'm thinking, well, of course! He always tells me when I'm wrong or when I've sinned. But does He actually just want to talk with me? Does He just want to tell me something other than "straighten up!"? Those statements send more like my earthly father.

I guess I'd have to say, about hearing the voice of God or the voice of Jesus, that I don't hear voices from heaven. One thing I do consider to be "the voice" is when I wake up with a song I have been singing in my head all night or a Scripture I find myself reciting all night. I usually google the lyrics or look up the verses.

One night it was Lou Christie's "I'm gonna make you mine." I hadn't thought of that song for years. Now I love that song. It encourages me that God is continuously pursuing me, working day and night to make me His. He is committed to drawing me closer and closer to Him. He's so in love with me that He's standing in line waiting for me to come to Him. He will never give up on me. His commitment to me is like an indestructible force. Yes, He's gonna make me His, He's gonna make me His.

So imagine my concern when I woke up after *Yea though I walk through the valley of the shadow of death ...* running through my head all night. Psalm 23:4

My first thought: who else is going to die today? Another one of my children? Me? My wife?

I went to the Bible to read Psalm 23. Okay, maybe it's just a shadow of death: a tragedy, an injury, maybe a stroke or heart attack. Still not so good. There are so many things to fear, especially when you let your mind run wild.

What do you fear? Maybe you fear another child dying, or maybe getting sick, or running out of money, growing old, or nobody coming to visit you when you do, or your spouse dying, or your only friend dying? Or even your own death? The possibilities are endless!

I re-read Psalm 23. *Even though ... I will not fear ...* But I was fearful. What are some "shepherd" verses that could help me?

> Psalm 78:52,53 *He led them like sheep, He guided them, He led them safely, so that they did not fear.*

> Isaiah 40:11 *He will tend, He will gather, He will carry, He will lead.*

> John 10:11 *I am the Good Shepherd. The Good Shepherd lays down his life for the sheep.* Verse 10: *The thief comes only to steal and kill and destroy; I came that you may have life and have it abundantly.*

If it has to do with stealing, killing or destroying, it is the work of the devil. If it has to do with life, it is the work of Jesus.

So, here I am today, a couple years later, wondering if that Psalm in the night wasn't meant for me today, as I sit here struggling with having my cancerous prostate removed, and still having an elevated PSA. T3b if anybody knows what that means.

I suspect that randomly turning to that particular journal entry today is God's plan, and His way of pointing me back to a happy heart. Maybe you, too, have had things come into your life that have taken away your happiness, or maybe have led you into fear and dread. Seek His voice. Listen to His voice. He does have words of encouragement for you today.

To trust in Him is to <u>not</u> expect that evil will come my way. To trust in Him is to <u>not</u> expect that bad things are just waiting to happen. Sure, trouble will come. (Jesus said, *in the world you will have tribulation, but take courage I have overcome the world.*) But because the Lord is my Shepherd I can, we can, fear no evil. Instead, trust that He is for you and His plans are for good, not for evil.

To trust in evil is to not trust in God. God, who is full of redemption and full of goodness has blessings for us, not evil. As I turn my mind back to the time of Josiah's death I keep reminding myself: the greatest test of faith in times of trouble is to believe that God is good; that in the midst of life's troubles, believe that He has good planned for us, because He does.

Psalm 23:4 may say, *Even though I walk through the valley of the shadow of death,* but it also says, *I will fear no evil.* Verse 5 declares that He prepares a banquet for us in the presence of our enemies … our cup overflows. Verse 6 encourages us that, when we walk in the dark and hear a noise and think, "Evil, is that you following me?" that we can hear the response, "No, it's just us, Goodness and Mercy."

Knowing this we can agree with Psalm 112:1-7, that we will not fear bad news. There may be bad things in life but God's words for us are good words. They are today's good news. Whatever comes our way, God is good, God can be trusted. He is *the lifter of our head.* He *makes His face to shine upon us.* He seeds our path with light and gladness. Today, declare: "I will sing for joy and be glad all day because God has satisfied me this morning with His lovingkindness."

On Your Own:

Psalm 12:6 What words do you want to hear from God today? If He were to give you a word for today, what would it be? Can you find that word in the Bible?

Prayer:

God, I am afraid of what might be around the next turn in the path of life for me. But I choose to take refuge in You, the Most High God, the Almighty. Instead of trusting evil, I choose to trust that you have good stored up for me. Open my ears to hear Your encouragement. Open my eyes to see the good that you bring my way <u>today</u>. Today is all I've got right now. Give me a song for my heart today.

Affirmation:

Today I hear god's words of encouragement, support, and direction.

Disappointed With God

It will come about at that time that I will search Jerusalem with lamps, and I will punish the men who are stagnant in spirit, who say in their hearts "The LORD will not do good or evil."
Zephaniah 1:12

I've been thinking about Zephaniah 1:12. God is singling out the men who are stagnant in spirit, or in their faith, and who believed in their hearts that God did not care enough to be involved. They believed that He does not answer prayer, at least not theirs.

Zephaniah records for the Lord: *It will come about at that time that I will search Jerusalem with lamps, and I will punish the men who are stagnant in spirit, who say in their hearts "The LORD will not do good or evil."* Or in other words, they say in their hearts, "We can pray but God isn't going to do anything." Forgive me, God, for sometimes believing that myself.

God answers SO many of my prayers. He comes to my rescue over and over again. Yet, I can get so hung up on one issue or one request that is not answered the way I think (or even claim and demand) that it should, and conclude it wasn't answered. Yet, God's way is so far beyond my comprehension, how could I ever imagine what He's actually trying to accomplish?

There have been times when I was angry that God did not answer my prayer, only to look back years later and see did He answer it. However He answered it in a far greater way. It was only my stubborn heart and my inflated ego that didn't recognize it at the time. He is always there, always listening, always answering, always working for my benefit, always improving my request to have an eternal everlasting effect on me and my world.

Here's a for instance: We pray that God would save a friend's marriage, change her heart regarding moving out. They say it's just a separation. But isn't a separation just a test drive on divorce and singleness?

We know that staying together is God's will. We quote Malachi "He hates divorce." But it's also His will that both of them face some of the issues that keep each of them from a fuller walk with Him.

Maybe these will never be faced while they're together. And if it comes to a final choice? Only God can answer and prioritize these issues. What will He do here? I believe one thing is evident: God is working in both their lives, and that is an answer to prayer. Do I know His top priority for their lives? Do I conclude that He doesn't care enough to answer my request, to take my recommendation? Or should I conclude that maybe He has priorities that I don't even know about?

Back to the issue of: Do I truly believe that God will do something, or am I convinced He has done nothing and will do nothing? Do I interpret my "unanswered" prayer as God's statement that He's not interested in helping me right now? Dare I think that my issue isn't important enough to warrant His attention? Has He rejected me and my request?

In Mark chapter 9, the man asking Jesus to heal his son from the spirit that throws him in the fire and into the water to destroy him, said, *If You can do anything …* Jesus' answer is pretty amusing: "*If You can?*" I can see Him smiling as He says that. Then He says, *All things are possible to him who believes.*

Can you partly believe something? I mean, it seems to me that either you believe something or you don't. Can you partly believe that God can do anything? Maybe so.

The child's father said, *I do believe, help my unbelief.* I think that's where faith abides, somewhere between belief and unbelief (which is not the same as disbelief). In Mark 6:6 Jesus wondered at the people's disbelief. He didn't marvel at their lack of faith, or their difficulty in believing something so amazing that only God could make it happen. No, he wondered at their refusal to believe.

When I discover that God has ignored my wise counsel and I observe that my prayers don't appear to be answered, do I conclude that I didn't have enough faith? Or did I waver in my faith? Or because I did _____ (fill in the blank with something I did wrong), He won't grant my request? Maybe I need to pray harder, or even shout when I pray. Maybe not enough people are praying. There's got to be a password here somewhere.

Jesus' disciples failed to cast out a spirit because, as Jesus said *this kind can only come out by prayer and fasting.* Maybe that's it, I need to fast.

Is greater faith a greater refusal to doubt? I don't think so. Maybe greater faith is a greater insight into what God wants to do right now. Or maybe it is greater insight into His will, His plan. Or maybe it is just greater humility to accept His plan over our plan.

I have prayed that God would heal my hearing, my spiritual hearing. Eight or nine months ago I received a diagnosis of prostate cancer. I say it was a diagnosis and not something "I have" because my attitude is: "It's not mine and I'm not going to keep it!"

My first line of defense any time I am sick is to ask God for healing in Jesus' Name. I have received divine healings quite a number of times. So when I received this diagnosis, I immediately had myself anointed with oil and prayers made for healing made on my behalf, twice. I even confessed my sins like James said to do.

So you can imagine my disappointment when I eventually opted to have my prostate removed, and yes, it was still cancerous. And there were some cancer cells found outside the prostate. I was quite angry with God and told Him how he had disappointed me and let me down. I declared, "Either Your promises to answer prayer are true or they're not. How can they possibly be true part of the time?"

I think I was trying to shame God into granting my request. (Good luck with that!) The only response I could discern was "Are you willing to trust Me?" I'd forgotten about my "hearing" request because this seemed so much more important, only to discover that He has been busy healing my hearing.

I cannot believe that God will do <u>nothing</u> in answer to my prayers. In the midst of my struggle I looked back in life and realized that there were other times in the past when He answered prayer, but not to my expectations. My expectations are what disappoint me, not God. The disappointment comes from being so focused on my plan that I refuse to see or accept His plan. I concluded that what God wants to do goes beyond my "fix my body" prayer. God doesn't want to do this for me. He wants to do it with me. He wants to do all of life with me, not just grief, not just cancer, but all of life.

My healing from grief was anything but instantaneous, yet it was miraculous. I found I couldn't wake up every morning and just pray "fix me, God." We had to do it together. A bit of crying mixed with His mercy. A bit of trouble mixed with His deliverance. A bit of gloom mixed with His joy and gladness. A bit of struggling in the Scriptures mixed with His revealing of Himself to me.

Day by day. Seeking, finding. Asking, receiving. Knocking, opening. Every day, putting on the new self who is being renewed to a true knowledge, according to the image of the One who created me. Colossians 3:10

The bottom line is that God loves us so much that He wants us to get to know Him, the real Him, not the "him" we have created in our minds. That may mean that life is not always what we wish it would be.

On Your Own

Romans 5:5, Romans 10:11 How do you reconcile these verses with disappointments you have had with God?

Prayer

Lord, I confess I have been disappointed. My disappointment has been over You not answering my prayers the way I believed You would or when I believed You would. I accept that my expectations have gotten in the way of seeing things from your perspective, but frankly, that's so hard to do. Open my eyes and my heart to accept <u>Your</u> answer.

Affirmation

Today my eyes are open to God's answer to my prayers.

Ebenezer (Not Scrooge)

Then Samuel took a stone and set it between Mizpah and Shen, and named it Ebenezer, saying, "Thus far the LORD has helped us." 1 Samuel 7:12

In 1 Samuel 7 we find Samuel leading the Israelites in a time of confession, repentance, and sacrifice. It was at that time, while they were worshiping the Lord, that the Philistines chose to gather their army together and come against Israel. 1 Samuel 7:10, *As Samuel was offering up the burnt offering, the Philistines drew near to battle against Israel.*

Before our son, Josiah, killed himself I had a season of closeness to the Lord that lasted for several months. It seems that some times God draws us close to Him to strengthen us for what is about to come. Not that whenever I draw close to Him, evil is on it's way, but He does love us enough to give us the strength and faith to be victorious in life.

This is what was happening with the Israelites. They had drawn near to Him, and when the Philistines attacked, they had the faith to call upon Him for help. We read that, *The LORD thundered with a great thunder on that day against the Philistines and confused them, so that they were routed before Israel.*

After the victory, Samuel set up a stone of remembrance, and named it Ebenezer, so that whenever an Israelite passed by that stone, it was a reminder of the great victory God had wrought for them.

Prior to our son's death I had never journaled. But from the time of Josiah's death until now I have journaled regularly. For a while it was sporadic but three or four years ago I began to write down at least three things I am thankful for every day. Some days it is brief, like "I'm thankful that yesterday is over." Other days I go on and on for an entire page.

A short while ago I began reading through some of my journals, just looking back. I was surprised by how many gifts and deliverances and answers to prayer and great family moments I had written about. This is kind of my Ebenezer, my rock of remembrance, *Thus far the LORD has helped me.*

I encourage you, like I encourage everyone I can, to journal on a regular basis. Write down anything that God has been doing for you or showing to you. Many things are seemingly small, like realizing I was texting when I shouldn't have been, and God kept me from running someone over. Well, it certainly wouldn't have been small if He hadn't done that for me.

Here's the funny thing: we can have blessing after blessing come our way. Then something bad happens and we're all, "God, won't you help us?" "God, I'm so down, show me some good!"

What I'm saying is this: Write down every gift, every victory, every positive moment, every good thing God brings into your life. When trouble comes you way, which it will; or when you're feeling down, which you will: or your day just seems dark, pick up your journal and begin reading through all the wonderful things God has done for you and for your family.

You will find your heart filled with joy and thanksgiving. You will find that your spirits are lifted, and that you can begin praising the Lord again. Put on some worship music, and I'll bet God will bring along a song that expresses the song in your heart so that you can sing along with it!

On Your Own:

Read all of Psalm 103. In verse 2, what had lifted David's heart and inspired him to write this wonderful psalm? If you want an extra-credit assignment: Write your own Psalm 103 and personalize it. For instance, instead of "who heals all your diseases," you may want to write, "Who has restored our family." Or instead of "He made known His ways to Moses," you may want to write, "He showed us what to do."

Prayer:

Lord, I'm so prone to forget the many amazingly good gifts you have given me in the past. Forgive me for such a short memory. Help me, even right now, to review the deeds of compassion and kindness you have done for me.

Affirmation:

I am enjoying filling my gratitude bank with every small and large blessing I see throughout the day, today.

Salt is good

Jesus said, "Everyone will be salted with fire. Salt is good."
Mark 9:50

That verse bothers me. At first I thought this was about turning lemons into lemonade. It's not. It's about trouble and redemption.

I'd rather read: "Everyone will be happy. Happiness is good." Face it: I don't like: *Everyone will be salted with fire.* But I can't change the truth of it.

I think about some who have been through the fire and it has destroyed them. I think of a particular someone who killed so many in the war that his life ended when the war ended. As Jesus said, their salt has become tasteless. No one wants to be around them.

Some fires are large, and burn us a lot, like your child's death. The burn recovery takes years.

Some fires are small. They just burn us a little. They leave little scars.

We need to turn each of these into salt. We can't do that. Only the Lord can. We can only make them into lemonade. We can tell ourselves, "That's just what happens in life, get over it, make the best of it." God, on the other hand, wants to do much more than make the best of it.

God is a God of redemption. He can turn our fires into tasty salt. In fact, the stories of fires in the Bible are filled with God's redemption. That's what we need, a perspective of redemption. We need to learn or to figure out how to turn each trouble, each fire, over to God for redemption.

Now I find myself thinking of another someone who killed so many people in the war that he has dedicated his life to helping others survive and conquer life. That salt is good.

Here it is, today, Christmas Eve. How does that work today, with the broken toilet and the broken printer and the broken garage door opener? Ok, I do see it, Lord, with the broken garage door opener. My son, who can fix anything, is putting in a new one as a Christmas gift. Now, that's redemption.

God, help me see how redemption can take place through the printer and the toilet. Open my eyes to see the answer to that. Otherwise, what's the meaning in these fires? *In the world you have tribulation!*

On the one hand I think, "This is stupid, things break. Just pay to get them fixed." (Lemonade = a new toilet and new printer!)

On the other hand I find this is a key to living with joy: Asking for and searching for God's redemption in a bad situation, and then discovering it in the small fires every day.

Ps 90:14 - *Satisfy me in the morning with Your lovingkindness so that I may sing for joy and be glad all day long. Make me glad according to the days you have afflicted me, according to the years I have seen evil.*

On Your Own:

Mark 9:50 What are some good things that have happened in you, or positive changes that have taken place in you, or in your character or in your faith, in the aftermath of the Fire of Death?

Prayer:

Lord, You say fire is good. I say fire hurts. Help my attitude to be one of surrender to Your burn therapy. Open my eyes to see that *salt is good.* Redemption is good. Trusting You brings me joy. Hearing your voice in the morning brings me joy. Hearing your voice this morning will open my eyes to the redemption I'll find in today's fires.

Affirmation:

God is bringing good out of every trouble I encounter today.

Change?

If anyone is in Christ, he is a new creature; the old things passed
away, behold new things have come.
2 Corinthians 5:17

Two months after Josiah died, our good friends' daughter, Breanna
Joy, was killed in a car accident. To make it even harder, her sister
was driving. My wife and I were at the ER with Breanna's mom. I
was trying and trying to get her dad on the phone. My wife said
later, "I was kind of hoping he wouldn't answer so he could have a
few more moments before his life is changed forever."

Josiah's death has changed me in so many ways. It has changed my
perspective on life and what's important to me. It has changed my
perspective on God, and what's important to Him. I look at almost
everything differently now.

Leo Tolstoy said, "Everyone thinks of changing the world, but no
one thinks of changing himself." This may be true for everyone,
except God. He is always busy changing us.

Am I the product of all that I have experienced in life? I don't think
so. I think I'm the product of how I've responded to all that I have
experienced in life.

Someone said, "You cannot become something your are not
without changing what makes you what you are." Jesus said
something similar when He told us that new wine demands new
wineskins.

Most of us want both. We want to be something we're not
(whatever that might be: thin, wealthy, kind, neat, victorious, joyful
…) But we want to be that without stopping the things that make
us what we are.

Ps 51:12 *Restore to me the joy of Your salvation and sustain me with a willing spirit.* I want to be more joyful, but I can't be more joyful without giving up the things, the thoughts, the actions that take my joy away.

What is it that destroys your joy? What are the thoughts or opinions or desires that take your joy away? Are you angry with God? Has He treated you unfairly? Has He let you down? What about your rights and other's wrongs?

I tell my kids, "If you're always focused on what you don't have, you'll never be happy. But if you spend your energy being thankful for what you do have, you can find happiness."

I think the beginning of changing my outlook to a more positive, joyful one begins with gratitude. After a death it is not difficult at all to realize that everything I have in life could disappear in a moment. Everything I have is a gift from Him; even my loved ones. To surrender all of it to God, and appreciate them and the life I do have, is the entryway into the joy of the Lord. How can this be possible? With God all things are possible, even the impossible.

Lord, all that I have and own is a gift from You. Help me enjoy it all wisely and not hold on too tightly, for even when these are gone, there'll always be You.

Ps 52:1 *The lovingkindness of God endures all day long.* We need to hear that, Lord. We may not wonder if it is true, we may just need the encouragement and the reminder. Whatever becomes of today, Help me trust You.

On Your Own:

Psalm 50:23 To express gratitude to God in the throes of a broken heart, is a sacrifice, and not one He takes lightly. Begin today by writing down three things you're grateful for. When you've done three, go for ten. When you've done ten, go for 20. By the time you get over ten, you'll find your gratitude going way beyond, "I'm grateful I'm alive ..."

Prayer

Lord, I do want to be more joyful. I know that true joy comes from You. I know, too, that by remembering all the good You've brought to me, and all the good times I've had with my child, that joy will be easier to find. Fill my heart with thanksgiving today.

Affirmation

Today I am grateful for every good thing I can find. Joy is on my path today,

Christ in Me

The mystery which has been hidden from the past ages and generations, but has now been manifested to His saints, to whom God willed to make known what is the riches of the glory of this mystery among the Gentiles, which is: Christ in you, the hope of glory.
Colossians 1:26-27

I often hear of You, Jesus, as giving Your body as payment for my sins. Yet, today I saw - You gave Your soul as a ransom for many, and to reconcile all things to Yourself.

John 10:17 is translated *I lay down my life so that I may take it again,* yet the word translated "life" is the Greek *psyche,* "soul." The life He gave was not just His body, but His soul, the very essence of Who He is. A martyr is one who gives his body but not his soul. Jesus was not a martyr, but the Savior, who gave His body <u>and</u> His soul. He was the exact representation of the nature of the Father, the fullness of deity dwelled in Him.

When He said, *Into Thy hands I commit my spirit,* He didn't just surrender His body. He surrendered <u>all</u>, His body, His soul, His fullness of deity, to pay for my sins and the sins of the world. His soul was laid on the altar of sacrifice.

You see, I believe that when my son died, he laid down his life, his body, but his soul went into the hands of God and that God carried his soul, unmolested, into Heaven. But Jesus had faith to believe that even if He let His soul go and released His grasp on it, that it would be raised up again by the Power of God. Ephesians 1:19,20, *these are in accordance with the working of the strength of His might which He brought about in Christ when He raised Him from the dead.* This is the Christ in me, the hope of glory.

I want hope. I need hope. Hope enables me to see beyond today, into the future. Hope motivates me to sing and praise God for what He is going to do. Christ in me gives me this hope. With this hope I can look forward and not get stuck looking back.

Hope lifts me out of my nearsighted view of today. When I reflect on the prayers that I have lifted up for myself, my family, my life, my friends, my future, rather than praying them over and over again, I find I can praise and thank the Lord for answering them. I can focus on being grateful for all the wonderful things I anticipate from, through, and because of Him.

The more I think of Christ in me, the hope of glory, the more I understand that this is a (or <u>the</u>) major key to all of my Christian life, the key to Christianity. The apostle Paul clearly tells us this is the mystery that was hidden for ages, but now is revealed to us and in us.

I'm thinking:

Not Christ for me: being there to help me win at all the games I play in life or the battles I fight.

Not Christ available to me: always ready to come to my side when I "need" Him.

Not Christ before me: paving the way so that my life is smooth, opening doors for me.

Not Christ behind me: cheering me on, encouraging me to do whatever I think I should do.

Not Christ above me: looking down from "up there somewhere," helping me when He can.

Not Christ beneath me: doing my bidding until I'm ready to give Him proper place in my life.

Not Christ around me: my own little bubble protecting me from everything bad in life.

Christ in me: giving me life, breath, existence, strength, purpose, deliverance, protection, counsel, comfort, light, redemption, salvation, healing, hope. So that I can live today for Him and with Him. So that I can be (and I am) complete in Him. Yes, complete in You, Lord.

Is Christ in you, your hope? Maybe you are at a point on your journey where you still need to get on the path that leads to God and His incredible healing power. Here's the simple path: 1) There was separation between man and God that began in the Garden of Eden, and that has afflicted every human since then. We all sin. 2) God reconciled the world to Himself through Jesus Christ. His life of faith, His death and resurrection opened a path for us to find our way back to Him. For every human on earth He has made everything right with God the Father. 3) Now it's our turn: Be reconciled to God … come back home. This is done by simply admitting that I have sinned and been separated from God; and by asking Jesus to save me from the penalty and punishment of my sin. Thank Him, because this is the beginning of new life.

On Your Own:

Romans 15:13 What brings hope our way? Colossians 1:26,27 What do these verses say to you about where the power for perseverance and hope comes from?

Prayer:

Life is extremely empty without You. It is merely existence. May Your power work mightily in me today. I love Your presence. You in me. My hope for today.

Affirmation:

Because Christ is in me, I am hopeful today. I am replacing negative thoughts with hopeful thoughts.

Do I know His ways?

Do not Harden your hearts, as ... when your fathers tested Me. They tried Me, though they had seen my work. For forty years I loathed that generation and said they are a people who err in their heart, and they do not know my ways. Therefore I swore in My anger, they shall not enter My rest.
Psalm 95:8-11

Those in the wilderness erred in their heart because they had seen God's work but they did not know His ways. Backing up to verse 6: *Let us worship. Let us kneel. He is our God. He is our maker, we are his sheep. We are His people. So - today if you hear His voice, do not harden your heart as your ancestors did.*

Maybe I need to think about this some more: He condemned the Israelites for having seen His works for 40 years but not knowing His ways. This year (I journaled this in 2010), I have known the Lord for 40 years, since 1970. How well do I know His ways? I've seen His works for 40 years.

I have to admit there are times, maybe even too many times, when I've been afraid of hearing the Lord's voice. I've been afraid of what He'd say, or what He'd demand of me, or take from me, or of how He'd disrupt or change my life. If I <u>really</u> knew His ways would I ever feel like that?

Forgive me, Lord, for judging Your plans, Your character and Your intentions based on my own character or nature. Forgive me for thinking that you are like me, or even like my father.

All His ways are good, righteous and filled with mercy and lovingkindness. I confess, even after realizing this and thinking about it, that I am a bit afraid of His voice still. But I do pray and ask Him to help me, or enable me, to see and trust His ways, not just His works. Help me to not err in my heart.

I have wondered at why Jesus didn't declare Himself more clearly to the Jewish leaders. After healing the man by the pool He testified to the Jewish leaders, *If I testify about myself, it is not true.* In other words, "If I come saying, 'I am the Christ' without evidence, my testimony is not true."

So He gave them the testimonies of 1) John the Baptist, John 5:33-35 *John testified to the truth.* 2) His works, John 5:36 *My works testify that I do the works of the Father.* 3) The Father, John 5:37-38 *The Father has testified of me.* 4) The Scriptures, John 5:39-47 *The Scriptures, specifically Moses writings, testify about Him.* He finishes His lecture with, *If you do not believe the writings of Moses, how will you believe Me?*

Why didn't Jesus come testifying about Himself? For the same reason He was upset with them in the wilderness. The Jewish leaders had seen His works for 3 years but still didn't know His ways. They were to be looking for Him, knowing the signs, knowing what to look for, knowing His ways. If they knew His ways they would have known He was Messiah.

The Lord's ways are always filled with love and compassion and goodness. I know this. I just need to trust it more. When life is crap, I can trust His ways rather my view of what happened, because I know His ways. His ways are filled with redemption, with overcoming

I know, and I believe, that He doesn't hurt us so He can help us. He doesn't afflict us so He can heal us. He doesn't make our lives miserable so that e will beg for deliverance. In fact, more often than I realize, He doesn't even force us to suffer the consequences of each of our stupid decisions. He is always for us and never against us.

In Psalm 100, this is how we are to enter His gates with thanksgiving: *give thanks to Him, bless His name, for the LORD is good; His lovingkindness is everlasting and His faithfulness to all generations.*

To all generations. To my generation. To your generation. To the generations of your parents and grandparents. To your children and their children. His faithfulness spans every generation, every culture, every moment. Yes, He is always dependable because it is His nature to be dependable. Confess it. Place faith in it. Live by it. This is your key to a new song. Psalm 27:13, *I would have despaired had I not believe that I would see the goodness of the Lord in the land of the living.*

The best thing for us, when we don't understand what God is doing, is to trust His ways. Trust what you know about how He does what He does. Trust His character. His ways are deep and undiscoverable. His ways may not appear good as we define good, but they are glorious. Trust His ways.

On Your Own:

Isaiah 55:8,9 When we wonder how God could possibly allow some things to come our way, what can we be sure of?

Psalm 147:17 What are two things we can know when it comes to the ways of God?

Psalm 145 Read this psalm and write down what it declares to you about the ways of God.

Prayer:

Heavenly Father, the Great I AM, Your ways are beyond understanding. There is so much in life I cannot control and cannot figure out, so I am throwing myself upon You, Your character, Your ways, which are higher than mine. I trust that. I confess it. I place faith in it.

Affirmation:

Today my eyes are open to seeing the goodness of the Lord.

Does Faith Always Work?

If I have all faith, so as to remove mountains …
1 Corinthians 13:2

I had definitely been spending too much time away from my office: running, biking, ignoring my business. So I hired this gal who was supposed to be a fantastic marketer. She had what I thought was a great marketing plan. She promised to make 50 marketing calls a day! She said her goal was 90 new clients.

At the time I had over 200 clients, so I thought that 90 might have been a little too optimistic. So I halved it, and began praying that God would bring us 45 new clients. A couple months later I remember praying to God: "Perhaps I didn't speak clearly enough. I said '45 new clients' not '4 to 5 new clients.'"

Maybe you've prayed for your child's health, or for their recovery, or for their healing, or just that God would enable them to live, and you've been disappointed. Does faith always work?

The Apostle Paul said, *God has allotted to each a measure of faith.* (Romans 12:3) It seems that Paul is indicating that some <u>do</u> have a stronger measure of faith than others. Did you not have enough faith?

I think everybody wants huge faith. We all want the faith to ask, to believe for, to receive whatever our heart desires, or whatever we believe God should be doing in, for and around us. Maybe what we really want is faith to control God, or faith to use God to control our situation. How often are our prayers an attempt to remain in control of a situation or an attempt to bring the uncontrolled under control?

There have been times in my life when I expressed to God my displeasure that He didn't take my good advice, that He had really disappointed me by not answering my request. But God knows we are not God and we don't have all wisdom and all knowledge, and not all of our desires, dreams, hopes and best ideas are righteous. So he doesn't give us "all faith." I don't think He ever gave anybody *all* faith.

I have an Evangelist friend who once said that God wasn't answering his prayers because his faith had outpaced his maturity. In other words he said he was asking for things he was not really mature enough to receive. I'm not sure that's true. Maybe his dreams or his vision, outpaced the maturity of his faith. It's almost like saying his vision outpaced God's. Maybe it was <u>his</u> dream, <u>his</u> vision, and not God's. But at the time faith wasn't working for him.

Faith works. Could I say, "Faith always works?" So is the "faith that does not work" something else? Hope? Belief in my idea? Trust in my vision? Desire rooted in my dream for my life and my family? An earnest longing for what I see as "good"? Maybe, but here's the hard part of my Christian life: being able to know which is which, which is what I want for my life and which is what God wants for my life.

Faith can be as simple as asking God for a boon, believing He may grant it just because He is good and loves to do good things for us, just like we like to do good things for those we love. I like that word, boon. Don Quixote used it. He was quite the visionary.

How much faith does that take? Not much really, just enough to believe in His love, enough to believe in the finished work of Christ on the cross. Just believing that God adores me and wants to shower me with affection. Does it take <u>more</u> faith to spare my child's life? I don't think so. But sometimes it does take a lot of faith to believe that God's plan, which is not all about me and my family (which may not include saving my child's life), is good, is best. Faith always works.

Trust His character. It does take a lot of faith to say to God, "I don't like what happened, or what's happening, or how things have turned out. But I choose to trust You. I choose to believe, like the song says, 'You're a good good Father.'" That's faith that works every time. Peace is God's gift to us every time we choose to trust Him (Isaiah 26:3). Having peace in my heart brings a song to my life.

On Your Own:

Romans 10:17 Does faith come from the bottom of my heart? Does it come from my greatest desires? Does it come from being good and doing good? Where does it come from?

Prayer:

I do trust You. I do believe that you adore me, my family, my child. I can have faith for that. I may still be really upset over the requests you seem to have ignored. But right now I declare that I trust that You know what's best, and that You will redeem the affliction, death and evil that has come my way. You will turn it into good. I cast myself upon your lovingkindness and goodness, knowing that You will turn my lament into a song of joy.

Affirmation, or My Expression of Faith Today:

I choose to believe that God is always good. My heart is filled with worship and gratitude today. Bless the Lord, O my soul.

Grief and Sorrow According to God

For godly grief brings a change of mind (repentance) that leads to salvation and leaves no regret, but worldly sorrow brings death.
2 Corinthians 7:10

Big Sky Bible College closed in 1983, bankrupt. I was a teacher there that last year. It goes without saying that this was a difficult year for the President of the college. During some of his darker days I made a plaque for him with these words from 2 Corinthians 4

Afflicted (pressed, troubled) in every way, but not crushed.

Perplexed (without resources, in want, embarrassed), but not despairing (neither utterly at a loss nor destitute of resources).

Persecuted (put to flight, harassed), but not forsaken (abandoned and helpless).

Struck down (thrown to the ground), but not destroyed (useless, ruined, lost).

Always carrying about in the body the dying of Jesus, so that the life of Jesus also may be manifested in our body.

Fifteen years later, when Josiah died, I received the plaque from him in the mail. He had kept it all those years, and now it was my turn to claim those truths for me and my family.

How does worldly sorrow produce death? Hopelessness, despair and emptiness. Sometimes I think, "When I get to heaven, do I want to tell my child, 'Your death destroyed me'?" That would be worldly sorrow producing death.

Godly sorrow or grief brings a change of mind, and change of perspective. And that leads to life that frees me from regret. Regrets may never disappear, but they do not need to control me.

When you feel sorrow, guilt, or regret, and there's no change of mind (repentance); no choosing to learn to view it from God's perspective, it works death. In other words, it crushes you into the ground. Paul says in 2 Corinthians 7 that changing how we view life, death, guilt and grief produces life.

Because of God's Spirit within us, we have the choice, the opportunity, the option, to change our mind about our situation, our trouble, our sin, our regrets. This change brings about life and freedom from regret … *leading to salvation without regret.*

So, grieving, literally "according to God," or "godly grieving" will produce life. Grieving without God will produce death.

The reason we have our life in "earthen vessels" is so that Jesus may shine in our hearts, giving the light of the knowledge of the glory of God, so that it is obvious to all who know us that the power (the power to survive, the power to turn darkness into light, death into life) is from God and not of ourselves. You can't do that on your own.

This is why, in the darkness, our light will shine. *The light shines in the darkness, but the darkness will not overtake the light.* (John 1:5) So, we can be afflicted, but not crushed; struck down, but not destroyed. The light and life that shines from us will not be from ourselves, our own power, but from God. The victory will not be our victory, but His victory. The new song in our heart will not be our song, but the song of life!

On Your Own:

2 Corinthians 7:4 Is it possible, and, is it God's plan, for you to have joy? Even in the midst of affliction, what kind of joy can you have? If it has been a few years since your child's death, write down how you would compare your level of joy now with a year ago?

Prayer:

Frankly, Lord, it is scary to think of darkness coming into my life so that Your light may be manifested. When I think about this too much it causes me to worry and be afraid. Yet I try to, no I choose to, trust you with my future and my family's future. I choose to trust that You will allow into my life only what fits Your plan for goodness. *I have no good but Thee.* (Psalm 16:2) I trust that I will see the goodness which You have stored up for me. (Psalm 31:19)

Affirmation:

Today I am exercising my ability and my God-given power to choose my state of mind. I choose victory over my circumstances. (Proverbs 23:7, Psalm 73:16)

The Power

We are afflicted in every way, but not crushed; perplexed, but not despairing; persecuted, but not forsaken; stock down, but not destroyed.
2 Corinthians 4:8,9

I can remember feeling: "God, I say I trust you, but I'm not so sure anymore. What you allowed to happen has nearly destroyed me. How could You have done that? It has caused me to question your goodness and your kindness. I want to believe in your goodness, but that's a little difficult right now. You're going to have to do a miracle to keep me going."

This is me (2 Corinthians 4): Afflicted in every way, but not crushed; doubting & confused but not despairing; harassed & molested, but not abandoned; struck down, but not destroyed. Remember this: your faith, as weak as it may seem, is stronger than your actions and your feelings.

In your grief and anger you might say and do things to God, and to others, that you regret. You may question God's goodness, or His ability to save, or His power or even His desire to stop evil. But your faith can, and will, remain intact. You might be like Peter, who, when numerous disciples of Jesus were leaving him, and Jesus asked him if he was going to leave too, said: *Lord, to whom shall we go? You have the words of eternal life!* If you think about it, where else can you go?

In that same section of 2 Corinthians 4, I also read, *We have this treasure in earthen vessels, that the surpassing greatness of the power may be of God, and not from ourselves,* I wondered: What power? Power for what? And why is it not just power, but great power; and not just great power, but surpassing great power. It is because I need a miracle, and yes, God delivers miracles.

In Jesus I have:
The power to survive.
The power to not be consumed or destroyed by grief.
The power to overcome; to come back, to heal.
The power to sing again.
The power to laugh again.
The power to be joyful again.
The power to look past the things that are seen (because they are terrible / troubling / overwhelming / temporary) to see the things that are not seen (because they are eternal).

And beyond all this He gives:
The power to manifest life instead of death.
The power to spread grace and light and life rather than darkness and despair.
The power, as Jesus said to Peter, to *strengthen your brethren.*
In other words, the power to truly live; to hear His lovingkindness in the morning; to see my day's path sprinkled with light and gladness; to have enough joy to share with others.

Yes, Brother, this is you: afflicted but not crushed ... always carrying about the dying of Jesus so that you can manifest the life of Jesus in your body. This is so next-to-impossible that it does take surpassingly great power from God Himself. The life we live is no longer ours, but it is Christ's, who lives in us.

On Your Own:
2 Corinthians 4:7-10 If there is purpose in us being human, and suffering the same things all humans suffer, what is it?

Prayer:
Lord, I don't believe that you manipulate evil to make good come about. But somehow You do permit evil to exist in this world, and somehow You do squeeze good out of it all. Help me to be part of that good that is delivered to the world today.

Affirmation

Today I am looking for an opportunity to be the instrument of good in someone's life.

Fierce

He who dwells in the shelter of the Most High will abide in the shadow of the Almighty. I will say to the LORD, 'My Refuge and my Fortress, my God in Whom I trust!' … He will cover you with His pinions, and under His wings you may seek refuge; His faithfulness is a shield and bulwark.
Psalm 91: 1-4

I recently memorized Psalm 91. I used to think, because it was quoted during Jesus' temptation, that it was about the Messiah, and not for me. But as I read it a while back, I began to ask, "Is this Psalm for me, Lord? I think it is!" So I memorized it. When I returned from vacation, a copy of a book about Psalm 91 was waiting in the mail for me that my sister-in-law had sent. Then on Sunday the Scripture reading in church was Psalm 91. Then my niece's daughter memorized Psalm 91 for "extra credit" at Bible camp. Ok, it is for me. It is for you, too. It's for any believer who chooses to seek refuge in the shelter of the Most High God.

We had these robins nesting in a tree just a few feet from our deck. We have lots of birds around. When some of them would land in the tree near the nest to see what's happening with the Robin Family, the robins ignored them. Even the humming birds would hover inches from the nest for twenty or thirty seconds, just watching. But when a blue jay or magpie would come anywhere near, the robins went into action.

They attacked these predators with such ferocity! The robins refused surrender their eggs or babies easily. They would chase, dive, attack, and scream.

They made me pray, "Lord, just as fiercely, please attack the enemy who has afflicted my soul, punish him for attacking my family. Afflict him worse than he has afflicted me. Attack him and send him running. Remember Your words in Psalm 91:3,4 *For it is He who delivers you from the snare of the trapper and from the deadly pestilence. He will cover you with His pinions, and under His wings you may seek refuge. Colossians 1:13, He rescued us from the domain of darkness and transferred us to the kingdom of His beloved Son."*

Continuing my prayer to the Lord I declare, "I belong to the Kingdom of Light, not darkness! Let me see light today. I take refuge in the shadow of Your wings until destruction passes by (Psalm 57:1). In this shelter, teach me to sing for Joy (Psalm 63:7). While You are busy attacking the enemy for me, put a song in my heart this morning and satisfy me with Your lovingkindness so that I may sing for joy and be glad all day (Psalm 90:14)!"

I'm surprised as I use my Bible app to look up verses that talk about being in the shadow of God's wings. There are so many. Here's a few:

- *In the shadow of Your wings I will sing for joy!*

- *Like an eagle that stirs up its nest, that hovers over its young, He spread His wings and caught them, He carried them.*

- *The children of men take refuge in the shadow of Your wings.*

- *Be gracious to me O God. For my soul takes refuge in You and in the shelter of Your wings.*

How often in the past have believers chosen to take shelter there and found what they were looking for? How often have they found that God is faithful and powerful and eager to rescue?

I think, "Lord, I don't know what's really happening to me and around me, or why. I don't know what You're going to do with me or for me, or even if You are going to do anything for me, although I don't know why You wouldn't, You always have before. I choose to say and declare that You are good and that You have good planned for me and my family today, tomorrow and on into whatever future You've planned for us. I will do what I can with what I've got!" Such a declaration lifts my soul and my head to focus on today. Like I said, I'll do what I can with what I've got. And what I've got is: today.

On Your Own:

Read Psalm 91. Write down as many things as you can find that declare how God is going to help you and lift your spirits today.

Prayer:

Fill my heart today with songs of joy and praises of thanksgiving. Give me a dependent heart that knows the sanctuary of Your wings.

Affirmation:

Turn to the Lord and declare, "I belong to the kingdom of light, not darkness! Let me see light today. I do take refuge in the shadow of Your wings until destruction passes by. (Psalm 57:1) In this shelter, teach me to sing for Joy. (Psalm 63:7) Put a song in my heart this morning. Satisfy me with Your lovingkindness that I may sing for joy and be glad all day!"

Forsaken

*My God, My God, why have You forsaken Me? Far from my
deliverance are the words of my groaning. O my God, I cry by day
but You do not answer ... Yet You are holy!*
Psalm 22:1-3

Are there times when you feel forsaken? Times when you just don't
feel that God is there for you? Times when pain, difficulty or
trouble eclipses His presence?

Jesus experienced complete abandonment by the Father on the
cross. He expressed it when He fulfilled Psalm 21 by crying, on the
cross, *My God, My God, why have You forsaken me?* At that
moment the Father did something He said He would never do to
us: He forsook His own Son.

He says He will never forsake us because, for you and for me, He
forsook Jesus on the cross. Jesus laid, not just His life, but His soul
on the altar and God the Father abandoned Him, left Him alone.
Yet in that moment, and in the moments to follow, Jesus breathed
faith. Psalm 22:3, *Yet, You are holy ...* Even in His final moment,
His declaration, on his own, without the presence of His Father, as
a man, as a man without the Holy Spirit, in faith, was: *Father, into
Your hands I commit My spirit* (Luke 23:46). Although He was
abandoned, He resurrected and proclaimed victory over death and
evil *by the power of an indestructible life* (Hebrews 7:15).

He experienced the abandonment of the Father for me and for you,
so that we might experience the gift of: *I will never leave you nor
forsake you.*

So what about feeling abandoned or forsaken? The Apostle Paul said, *Persecuted but not forsaken; struck down but not destroyed* (2 Corinthians 4:9).

Like an iceberg, 90% of God's activity in our life, 90% of His blessings, are below the waterline, they are not easily observable. Not everything God does for us is to show us He loves us. He does these things because He loves us and has favor on us, whether we notice them or not.

God doesn't work on our behalf all day and night just so we notice this and thank Him. He obviously likes it when we do, but His love is such that He doesn't do it for the acknowledgement, but just because He loves us and favors us.

When we do see His blessings, His workings, we thank Him for them. Surely that is good. But much more than what we see is what He is constantly and consistently doing this. 1 Corinthians 13:4-7: *love does not brag and is not arrogant … it does not seek its own.* Yes, that would be God's love. His love does good because of love, whether I see it or not. Like an iceberg, God loves us so much that there's tons and tons of good He does for us every day, just because.

He causes the rain to fall on the just and the unjust. He is good, even to the evil and ungrateful. He is good to me, even when I am ungrateful. But being grateful opens the window to see not just the 10% above water, but some of the 90% below. Although we are blessed, the greater blessing is to see the blessings!

Grief is such a powerful emotion that can overshadow your sense of God's presence. To have a greater sense of God's presence begins by asking Him to open your eyes. Begin thanking Him for what good we do see. The longer the list of thanksgiving grows, the more we become aware of His activity in, around and for us. *Though the Lord is on high, He looks upon the lowly.* (Psalm 138:6)

On Your Own:

Psalm 119:83, Psalm 119:109, Psalm 119:141 When this psalmist was troubled, what saved his relationship with God?

Begin a practice of regularly writing down things for which you are thankful every day. Maybe even keep a Thankful Journal in which you keep a log of the things God is doing for you.

Prayer:

Thank You, Father, that You are with me, working on my behalf and my family's behalf day after day. Thank You that you have never forsaken me. You have always been right here for me, even when I don't think so. Thank You for all you do that I never see. Open my eyes. Give me a heart of gratitude.

Affirmation:

Today I have eyes open to blessings great and small that come from a loving and good Father.

O Love That Will Not Let Me Go

In this is love: not that we loved God, but that He loved us ...
1 John 4:10

Can I comprehend God's love for me? Somewhat, maybe. His love for me is so powerful that He was actually pleased to crush Jesus on my behalf (Isaiah 53:10, as well as the second half of the verse above, 1 John 4:10 - *He loved us and sent His son to be the satisfaction for our sins*). That's why I can only understand it somewhat. I want to understand it more. It seems to me, too, that part of knowing it deeply involves knowing how much I don't deserve it. When I feel I've let Him down is when I feel the least deserving.

So I say, "Lord, to know Your power is great. To be 'lifted up' is great. To know that I have an incorruptible inheritance is great. But what is really important to me today? To know You. To know and sense Your love. With every breath I take I want to recognize that I am breathing Your life in me and for me. I want to be aware that You think about me every moment of every day; that You plot my course and guide my steps; that every beat of my heart is You beating in me, for I have been put to death with Christ (Romans 6:8 and Colossians 3:3), and It is no longer I who live, but Christ lives in me."

Now that's something to be thankful for! *To know the love of Christ which surpasses knowledge, that you may be filled up to all the fullness of God* (Ephesians 3:19). To be filled to the fullness of God, how does that happen? How do we become rooted and grounded in love? How do we comprehend a love that is incomprehensible?

How would I gain that knowledge of His love anyway? By experiencing His power in my inner man; by knowing that He loves me and supports me when I'm in trouble, when I'm oppressed, when I'm depressed, when I'm wandering, when I'm searching, when I'm finding, when I'm struggling, when I'm hurt, when I'm worried, when I'm harried, when I'm happy, when I'm sad. When I'm confused or doubting, I can depend on His character - He is love.

To have faith that He loves me and helps me in every condition and every circumstance I could ever be in, is to know His love. To know that, no matter how deep the pain, His love is deeper still.

God has created this difficult and complex universe where good and evil plays out in each of our lives. This is an eternal universe in which, somehow, He has remained the "light." He has remained holy and pure. This is a universe in which, through no action of His own, I am assaulted by evil, by the reaping of my own consequences as well as the consequences of others' sins. Yet God in some marvelous way redeems me and my life and my situation through His love so that I know His love in each and every circumstance in a way that I could never have known it had the world been all sweet and beautiful and perfect.

By the world's imperfection, I know His perfection. By the world's cruelty, I know His love.

Oh the deep, deep love of Jesus

Oh the deep, deep love of Jesus
Vast, unmeasured, boundless, free
Rolling as a mighty ocean
In its fullness over me
Underneath me, all around me
Is the current of your love
Leading onward, leading homeward
To your glorious rest above
Oh, the deep, deep love of Jesus
'Tis heaven of heavens to me
And it lifts me up to glory
For it lifts me up to thee

On Your Own:
Matthew 13:44, and 45-46 Read this with the understanding that you are the treasure and the man who found it is God. What does this tell you about His love for you?

Prayer:
Father, I surrender to Your love. I have tried, without great success, to figure out You and figure out life. I believe You love me more than I can ever comprehend, and so today I trust Your love for me.

Affirmation:
I am trusting God's love for me today. I am watching for evidence.

I'm Sorry I'm So Needy

Not that we are adequate in ourselves to consider anything as coming from ourselves, but our adequacy is from God, Such confidence we have through Christ toward God.
2 Corinthians 3:4,5

I can remember coming to God in prayer, **again,** asking Him to help me. I felt so inadequate, so disabled when facing life. I didn't have the answers. I didn't have the energy. I didn't have the direction for one day, let alone the direction for life. I felt like this was becoming a perpetual thing for me.

I prayed to God, "Lord, I need You so badly today. I am sorry that I keep coming to You so needy, so inadequate. It seems like every day I am desperate for Your help." It was so clear to me right then, that God was saying to me: "You're okay. It is good that you come to me like this, because you <u>are</u> inadequate, and I AM <u>all</u> adequate. You are insufficient, and I AM <u>all</u> sufficient. That's the way it's supposed to be. That's the way you'll find true life, by being totally dependent on ME."

Psalm 116 begins with words I love to hear and dwell on: *I love the LORD because He hears my voice and my supplications. Because He has inclined His ear to me, I shall call upon Him as long as I live.* Then the Psalm goes on and on about how He has rescued me / us / King David:

> *He saved my life when death, Sheol, terrorized me.*
>
> *He saved my soul, saved me, when I was brought low.*
>
> *He dealt bountifully with me when I did not have peace.*
>
> *He rescued my soul from death.*
>
> *He rescued my eyes from tears.*
>
> *He rescued my feet from stumbling.*
>
> *He let me walk before Him when I was afflicted.*

So, *what shall I render to the LORD for all His benefits toward me?* Praise, thanksgiving, payment of my vows. I shall continuously call upon *the Name.* I shall continuously recognize my inadequacy and His adequacy; my inability and His infinite ability; my weakness and His strength; my poverty and His abundance; my falling and His upholding; my enslavement and His constant rescue; my lowness and His loftiness! Hallelujah Yah. (Take a look at the marginal notes in your Bible, "Praise the LORD" is the translation of "Hallelujah Yah"!)

My conclusion is the same as the Psalmist: Therefore I shall call upon Him as long as I live!

Whatever you need, He has it. Whatever you lack, He has it. Whenever you are empty, He has fullness. Whenever you are incomplete, He is complete. Whenever you are inadequate, He is adequate. Whenever you are insufficient, He is all-sufficient. <u>All</u> sufficient.

On Your Own:

2 Corinthians 3:5,6 Where does this adequacy come from? What does this have to do with the phrase, *but the Spirit gives life*? How does this affect how you live today?

Prayer:

Heavenly Father, Thank You for showing me that I cannot manage life on my own. I thought I could until it all came down around me. Now I know how it is possible to manage life, by depending completely on You.

Affirmation:

Today my eyes are open to seeing the Lord reveal His adequate provision and help for me and my family.

The Cure

Do return, O LORD; (how long will it be?) And be sorry for Your servants. O satisfy us in the morning with Your lovingkindness that we may sing for joy and be glad all our days. Make us glad according to the days You have afflicted us, and the years we have seen evil. Let Your work appear to Your servants and Your majesty to their children. Let the favor of the Lord our God be upon us; and confirm for us the work of our hands; Yes, confirm the work of our hands.
Psalm 90:13-17

Is the LORD's return he cure for the grieving? For the hurting? For the lonely? For the afflicted? For me? The Psalmist's cry starts with his admission that it seems like a long time in coming, *How long will it be?* I know I've felt that way. Eventually it will be.

The cure for right now? The Psalmist knows the drill: *Satisfy us in the morning with Thy lovingkindness that we may sing for joy and be glad all our days.* It must begin with seeking Him - seeking Him early and seeking Him often.

Our pastor said that we learn very little about life from pleasure. The real lessons are learned in the pain. Only by seeking the Lord early and often can we change our perspective, brighten our outlook. Only then can we develop a view of life like His.

This Psalm is a prayer of Moses. He knows the start of the best day is when he has been satisfied in the morning with God's lovingkindness, His unending commitment and covenant of love. "Show me the love" is a fair request of God - that is, if we're willing to see it.

It is through God's personal revelation that I come to realize and accept that the bottom line to all of life, for me personally is: I have Jesus. I may lose everything in life, maybe even like Job, in the blink of an eye, but I'll still have Jesus. Because of this everything will be all right. It certainly will not always be good, but it will be all right. *I shall not be greatly shaken* Psalm 62:2.

It is from the exercise of finding Him early and often, of seeking to somehow touch Him, to receive a word of guidance or instruction or encouragement from Him for the day, that our joy and gladness comes for the day.

It is then that we begin to live off of verses like the one above from Psalm 90. Or verses like Psalm 4, *Many are saying, 'Who will show us any good?' Lift up the light of Your countenance upon us, O LORD! You have put gladness my heart, more than when their grain and new wine abound. In peace I will both lie down and sleep, for You alone, O LORD, make me to dwell in safety.*

Or like Psalm 73, *Whom have I in heaven, but You, and besides You I desire nothing on Earth. My flesh and my heart may fail, but You are the strength of my heart and my portion forever … as for me, the nearness of God is my good; I have made the Lord GOD my refuge, that I may tell of all Your works.*

Or like Psalm 109, *With my mouth I will give thanks abundantly to the LORD, and in the midst of many I will praise Him, for He stands at the right hand of the needy, to save him from those who judge his soul.*

Or like Psalm 103, *Bless the LORD, O my soul, and all that is within me, bless His holy name … He satisfies your years with good things so that your youth is renewed like the eagle.*

On Your Own:

Psalm 143:8-10 What is to gain by seeking Him early and often? Can you commit to doing just that?

Prayer:

Lord God, I find that the day is not worth living if I haven't found You and Your words of help, guidance, and encouragement for me. Help me be diligent to give You this time regardless of how the day presses upon me.

Affirmation:

Because You have satisfied me with Your lovingkindness this morning, I sing for joy and gladness all day today.

Rejoice

Rejoice in the Lord always, and again I will say, rejoice.
Philippians 4:4

Not too long after our son died I was at a gathering. Actually it was a reception after another funeral. A friend, who was also a grieving father, introduced me to another grieving father, as "another member of the club." This is the club we're all in. The club none of us ever thought about before, and never wanted to join, the club of grieving parents.

Before long, word gets out and soon you're introduced to this one, whose daughter was killed in a car accident, and that one, whose son killed himself, and on it goes. I care about these families, because I feel their pain. I know of the impossible days ahead for them.

But one day I said to my wife, "I am so tired of thinking, reading, writing, talking, hearing about death. I need LIFE to resound in my heart and mind. I need some sunshine after all the dark rain." I told the Lord the same thing.

The next morning the first verse I read was, *Praise is becoming to the upright,* Psalm 33:1.

Sometimes in Church I look around me and I am blessed by how beautiful everyone looks as they are praising the Lord in worship. As I worship, sometimes I look around at the lead worshipers, as well as others nearby and watch the joy and adoration they have for the Lord as they sing and praise. It puts such a smile on my face. Sometimes I laugh. Then I just have to praise more myself.

Philippians 3:1, and 4:4, *Rejoice in the Lord,* and *Rejoice in the Lord always.* It makes me think of my time in Bible college, being in the choir and part of the gospel team. I picture myself watching Mrs. Rupp smile as she led us in that chorus, "Rejoice! Rejoice! And again, I say, Rejoice!"

Psalm 32:11, *Be glad in the LORD and rejoice you righteous ones! Shout for joy, all you who are upright in heart!*

It makes me think, too how she would sing in church with her super high voice, harmonizing with the rest of the congregation. It sounded like angels were singing with us.

Psalm 33, *Give thanks with the Lyre, sing praises with a ten-stringed harp. Sing a new song,* and to me this day, that means a song of LIFE, sung and played with a shout of joy! Songs of deliverance, songs of life, songs of joy in the LORD, for He has done great things, and great are His thoughts towards me. He is good and does good.

His word is **upright**. **Upright** - Hebrew *yashat - the whole, everything, enough.* The Word of God is everything - to me, to us. His works are done in **faithfuness**. **Faithfulness** - Hebrew *emuwnah - firmness, steadfastness, fidelity, steadiness.* I read in Exodus 17:12 that Moses' hands were *steady* until the sun set. God's works are done with steady intention.

He loves righteousness and justice. The earth is full of His lovingkindness. **Lovingkindness** - literally a covenant of love. Look, today, and see His love, His mercy, His covenant of love being played out around you. Lord, give us eyes to see Your lovingkindness around us today!

Let all the earth stand in awe of Him. Look around you and let the awe of creation sink in. You may need to go someplace where you can actually see the wonders of creation. Do it. Or at least, scrutinize or meditate on the amazing creation: a hummingbird - how beautiful and amazing, your own eyes and ears - how could they have possibly evolved? No, this amazing, loving God created you with them. Or even a leaf, its intricacy and purposefulness.

It may be hard to make the connection, but the God who put it all together - the massive, the intricate, the invisible, the infinite, the incredible - is the same God who is giving you light and life today … For He spoke and it was done! He is speaking to you today and His word is: "live!"

Behold, the eye of the Lord is on those who fear Him, those who hope for His love, to deliver their souls from death. Our heart rejoices in Him because we trust in His holy name.

On Your Own:

Psalm 9:2, Psalm 71:23, Psalm 98:4 Find a song of praise for your heart today. Dig one out. Ask God to give you one. Sing it out loud; sing it in your heart all day. Don't wait for joy to arrive, put joy into your heart and mind today. You need it. He wants you to have it.

Prayer:

Lord, I needed that today. I will rejoice in You. I need to trust in Your Name: YHWH, I AM, and Your Name, Jesus, I AM SAVES. Yes, let Your lovingkindness, Your joy, Your gladness be upon me today!

Affirmation:

Because He has satisfied me with His lovingkindness this morning, I am singing for joy and gladness all day long. (From Psalm 90:14) Yes, twice in a row. It's a great affirmation!

It is Not Well With My Soul (But I Want it To Be)

Beloved, I pray that in all respects you may proper and be in good health, just as your soul prospers. 3 John 1:2

I remember a lot of days feeling like everything was all wrong. I felt like life was traveling North and South and I was heading East and West. I questioned every thought and every decision. Everything I did seemed wrong.

It's not like that so much any more. In fact, most days I am filled with peace and gratitude, happiness and blessing. But not today. Today as I listened to the hymn "It is well with my soul," I wanted to soak it in and have that feeling, but things just haven't felt right. My heart is heavy and I don't know why. I don't want to stay that way today.

As I read Psalm 25 I identify with the clash David feels between what he wants to be and what he is. He says, on the one hand: *The paths of the LORD are lovingkindness and truth to those who keep His covenant and His testimonies.* And then on the other hand, he wants to deal with what he knows about himself: *For Your name's sake, O LORD, pardon my iniquity for it is great.*

David is not the only one with that conflict. I know that to those who keep His ways, the promise is a path of lovingkindness and truth. But my iniquity is great and I need His pardoning to be on that path. I know I own a complete pardon through my Lord and Savior, Jesus Christ, but I don't always feel that way, or that I have adequately appropriated it.

So, I say to the Lord, "For Your name's sake, fill my heart with your love, your goodness, your forgiveness, your new life this morning. Cause my soul to abide in prosperity. Cause my mind to dwell on the <u>good</u> path you have for me today." And: "You declare that Your paths are full of lovingkindness and truth. I want to walk on that path today."

Your truth for today? That His path for today is full of good. He is constantly and consistently "right here" for you. So encourage your heart with these scriptures, they are your truth for today.

There are <u>so many</u> things in life that are out of your control. In fact, most things are out of your control. So thank the Lord and declare that you trust Him when He says that He will bless you and provide for you. Acknowledge to Him that you believe He will answer, He will heal, He will protect, He will redeem … to the 1,000th generation.

This is the generation of those who seek Him, who seek Your face. So, tell yourself, "Be certain. Believe these promises with certainty. Bank on them. Depend on them with your life, for they are true." They are true for you and for your family. God is not a man that He should lie. All the promises of God are <u>yes</u> and <u>amen</u>.

2 Corinthians 1:20-22, *For all the promises of God find their "yes" in Him (Jesus).* That is why we utter our "amen" to God for His glory. … Now He who establishes us with you in Christ and anointed us is God who also seals us and gave us the Spirit in our hearts as a pledge.

Acknowledging these truths will put us back on the path of "It is well with my soul!"

So, self, lift your head and open your heart *so that the King of Glory may come in! Who is the King of Glory? I AM, the LORD of Hosts, He is the King of Glory.*

On Your Own:

Psalm 51:6 Are you able to turn from your feelings to the truth?

Pick a truth that addresses a lie that is leading you to doubt God's good plan for you. Memorize it today.

Prayer:

Thank You, Lord, for being my light on this path. Thank You for reminding me that because You are for me and not against me, that it can be well with my soul.

Affirmation:

Goodness and lovingkindness pursue me and follow me all the days of my life. They pursue and follow my wife, my children, my grand children. I can say this because the blessing of the Lord is upon me to the 1,000th generation.

A Finished Product?

I am confident of this very thing, that He who began a good work in you will perfect it until the day of Christ Jesus.
Philippians 1:6

He who began a good work will perfect it, complete it. The work in me will be completed and I will be a finished product.

I think that to us humans, especially North American humans, a "finished product" seems to be a life well-lived with health on into old age. It means a successful business or career and a successful family, followed by a successful old age, climaxed with a heavenly and peaceful home-going.

When I think of Josiah dying at 15 1/2, or even of King David's child dying as an infant, or Stephen stoned to death as a young man, or of godly King Josiah the reformer dying at 39, or John the Baptist, dying at 30 or 31, I find myself questioning, "What is a finished product?" Are these lives "finished products" just as much as King David's life was, dying old and satisfied, or the aged patriarch Jacob, or the Apostle John still writing epistles at 90?

He who began a good work in you will complete / perfect it. I've always believed it will be true for me, but what about for my child? Was his life complete?

As a craftsman I want my finished product to be just right. I put the finishing touches on it before I show it to anyone. If my son, Josiah, was a finished product of God's work, then God's definition of a finished product is very different from mine; much more unseen, much more His project than mine.

Can I believe Philippians 1:6 for my son as much as I want to believe it for myself? I must.

In a man's house there are many vessels, some of gold and silver, some of wood and earthenware (2 Timothy 2:20). All the dishes in a man's house, and all the dishes or vessels in God's house, serve a purpose. They serve the Master's purpose. They are all used by Him.

I thank You, Lord, that my child served his purpose, and Your purpose, and that his life continues to serve Your purpose. His purpose lives on in me, in my family, in the world, in Your kingdom, and in Your household. I thought I was preparing him for life, but I discovered he was preparing me for life.

God's purpose is eternal. The value of His finished product lasts forever. It can have eternal impact because it had an eternal purpose. It was part of an eternal plan. The life of Abel, the first to die, had an eternal plan. God's word says his life still speaks today (Hebrews 11:4).

He who began a good work in you … Your child was His good work, not your good work. His life still speaks with an eternal voice. The value of your child's life, as a "finished product" lasts forever because it had an eternal purpose. His life was and is part of an eternal plan.

On Your Own:

Philippians 2:17 If you were to view your child's life as a drink offering poured out on the sacrifice and service of your faith, what would that mean to you? To your life? To your view of how to take the best of your child and multiply it for good?

Prayer:

Work Your work in me today. Help me be Your willing clay and to be about Your purpose. Show me how to multiply the good you had placed in my child. Thank You that You are using my child's life to teach me how to live. Thank You that my child's life can have an eternal impact on this world.

Affirmation:

I am becoming a better person because of the good my son/daughter left behind.

The Straight and Narrow

Enter ye in at the strait gate: for wide is the gate, and broad is the way that leads to destruction, and many be which go in thereat: Because strait is the gate, and narrow is the way which leads unto life, and few there be that find it.
Matthew 7:13,14

This Scripture is sometimes used to describe salvation. Some will tell you: "Walk the straight life, find the narrow path, and you'll find salvation." But the word is "strait" not "straight." This is the path that leads to life: going through the straits! I want life, real life, not just a happy existence.

I believe that, because of Josiah's death, I have been chosen to receive life. I'm not talking about eternal life - I've already got that. I'm talking about real life, abundant life. You, too, have been chosen by God to receive life. God is giving us an opportunity. He is shining a light on the path that leads to life. You can choose to take that path.

I came that you might have life, and that more abundantly. That path to life, Jesus said, is a difficult path with a narrow gate, and only a few find the way.

Have you ever had someone say, "Come over here, I want to show you something?" From where you were standing you could not see what they could see. You needed to go to where they were standing so you could see it.

When Josiah died, actually with every great loss, worldly life has been taken away from me. The life I thought I had was exposed to be the imposter. It was exposed for its real emptiness. This was exposed by God to show me the narrow and difficult gate.

I could not see the gate from where I stood prior to his death. God had to make me stand at death's door, where the view is different, to see the narrow and difficult gate - and it is difficult. Dealing with our child's death is the most difficult thing you and I have done to-date.

The passage through this gate is the path of trust and the path of constantly seeking Him. As I constantly seek Him, the faux life fades and the true life grows.

The wide gate is the one everyone is passing through. The other gate is narrow, the entrance is through difficulty, and it is not easily apparent, except to those who are looking.

"Strait" has the idea of being pressed or compressed into a small and difficult space. One does not pass this way without affliction. The doorway to life is the doorway of difficulty. The path of the grieving is not easy, but it is a path that can lead to life. This path is ours to choose.

"Narrow" means to be pressed by circumstances. Pressed, squashed, afflicted, hemmed in, troubled. Sounds like grief to me. Paul said he was *afflicted but not crushed … struck down, but not destroyed*. Why? So that the life of Jesus may be manifested in his body. *Therefore we do not lose heart but … we are renewed day by day*. I want that. I want to be newer, better, happier, more like Jesus, day by day.

Isaiah 30:20: *Although the Lord has given you the bread of affliction and the water of oppression, He, your Teacher, will no longer hide Himself, but your eyes will behold your Teacher. And your ears will hear a word behind you: "This is the way, walk in it."*

The path to life is found by searching. No one has to search for the broad path. Determine today that you will search until you find Him, every day. Search until you hear: *This is the way, walk in it.*

On Your Own:

Matthew 7:13,14, John 10:10 What does God have planned for those who persevere and make it through the narrow and difficult gate? Right now your vision may be narrow and your days difficult, but can you believe these verses enough to persevere?

Prayer:

Lord, I never signed up for "difficult." But I do want to find the gate that leads to life. Give me the courage to walk through this gate with You holding my hand.

Affirmation:

Tomorrow is what I make of today.

Life on other planets?

*O Lord, how many are Thy works. In wisdom Thou has made all of
them. The earth is full of Thy possessions.*
Psalm 104:24

Some wonder if there is life on other planets. I do not believe that
there is another race like mankind, unless it is perfect and doesn't
need redemption. I can't imagine the Son of God going from planet
to planet dying for sins! First for humans, then for Klingons, then
for Romulans … In fact, I believe God is often disappointed when
we fail to realize that all of this we see, looking up, looking down,
looking around; all of this He created for us. We are the
centerpiece of His creation.

I suppose it is possible that God has placed amazing creatures and
plants on other planets just for his own enjoyment and the
enjoyment of His angels. Yet to think of planets full of creatures
that are basically pets would be like living on an island with no one
to talk to but an aquarium full of fish or a sky full of birds, hardly
aware of your presence. Even if they are aware they couldn't
provide meaningful or stimulating or satisfying conversation.

And so, God, after He created all except mankind said, "It is good."
Then He spoke "let Us make man in Our image." After which he
said, "It is very good." All of creation is good. Only man is very
good.

What was one of the first things He did after He made man? He
walked with him in the garden. He did not communicate with any
of His creation until He made man.

It is clear that man without God is incomplete, for He is the very
breath in our lungs and the beating of our heart. He is the sustainer
of all life, therefore He knows if even a sparrow ceases to exist.

Somehow it seems that God maybe is not complete without man. Okay, blasphemy. I know He is complete without anything because He is God. He certainly could have existed on and on forever without ever creating a creature that could respond to His majesty. He could have, but maybe that was too boring for Him. He created angels to respond to His majesty. He gave them an opportunity at free will and one-third fell and followed Satan.

Yet there's something in the nature of angels for which He did not want to die. Unlike mankind, they were not made in His image. He was only willing to die for mankind. Now that the angels, apparently, are "confirmed" in holiness (or in wickedness), only man has the free choice of communing with Him or ignoring Him or even hating Him.

So what is it that God is looking for in creating mankind? Creatures who, by their own choice, honor Him. Creatures who are like God, knowing good and evil; like God, free in the expression of self; like God, able to destroy or save as an act of the will. Most of all, having God's infinite powers and characteristics in a finite fashion. Man is able to respond to God in a sentient manner, choosing good or evil.

The rest of the aquarium can respond in a limited way, but without the first-hand knowledge of good and evil. I have experienced evil, but I choose good. I have thought evil, done evil, seen evil, and in the death of my son, experienced evil. But I choose good.

Satan told Eve: "God knows that in the day you eat from it your eyes will be opened and you will be like God, knowing good and evil." How did he know that? Did God whisper that in his ear? Did God tell him that, so he would tell it to Eve?

Here is what I believe: God wants to populate heaven with creatures, humans, who know good and evil, just like He does, and who choose good, just like He does. The only way we can do this is by staying in close relationship with Him. Fellowship with Him is what we are created for. Immediately after creating Adam, God walked with him in the garden.

We have seen and experienced too much evil; greater evils and lesser evils. Death is the ultimate. It is the ultimate humiliation, the ultimate evil. We must refuse to let this evil paralyze us, or control us, or define us. We choose good, because we are made in God's image.

Choose to trust that God will talk with you, guide you, fix/redeem you, heal you, fill you with joy. Choose to develop a life-long close relationship with God. This is only possible through walking with Him day after day.

On Your Own:

Philippians 3:8-10 What was Paul's driving desire? On a scale of 1-10, how much is that your desire? What are you willing to do today to know Him better?

Prayer:

Lord, I choose to seek You today. I want to *hear Your lovingkindness in the morning so that I may sing for joy and be glad all day. Wait in silence for God only. From Him only is my salvation. Whom have I in heaven but You, and besides You, I desire nothing on the earth. My heart and my flesh may fail, but You are the strength of my heart and my portion forever.*

Affirmation:

I daily prioritize my quest to know God better.

Magnafluxed

So although I wrote to you, it as not for the sake of the offender nor for the sake of the one offended, but that your earnestness on our behalf might be made known to you in the sight of God.
2 Corinthians 7:12

Are there times when God uses difficult circumstances to teach us about *ourselves?* In the verse above, Paul explains that the instructions he wrote about the sinning church member were intended to teach the Corinthian church about themselves. (*That your earnestness … might be made known to you.*)

When I was in high school, my best friend, Rob's, father was a VP at Magnaflux Corporation. I learned this when his father got us deluxe tickets for the Indianapolis 500 race. Later, when I was a helicopter mechanic in the Army, I discovered what Magnaflux was all about.

Magnaflux Corporation had then, and still now, has the slogan, "Non-Destructive Testing." How does one find out if a critical bolt on a race car, or an aircraft, has a microscopic crack that will cause a failure without twisting and torturing it so that it breaks? They have a way. This is incredibly valuable because you can determine which parts are likely to fail without harming the part that is <u>not</u> likely to fail.

One thing I have learned about good and evil: the devil tempts, tests, and tries us with the clear purpose of destroying us. He came destroy (John 10:10). God will not tempt us (James 1:13); He will not test us with the intention of hurting or destroying us. He came to give us life (John 10:10). But He <u>will</u> test us, with the purpose of proving us, of proving our faith, to Him and, more importantly, to ourselves.

John 6:6, Jesus tested Philip, and we're told: *This He was saying to test him, for He Himself knew what He was intending to do.* Jesus already knew what was in Philip. He tested Philip so Philip could learn what was in Phillip.

Now I do not believe that my son's death came to us as a test from God. God does not inflict His people with trouble so that he can rescue them. But I do believe that in the wake of his death, and as a result of his death, the earnestness of our faith was made known to us. It has shown us where our real strength lies.

Right now you may not feel strong. You may not feel faithful. But I do believe that if you take time to reflect on your response to your child's death, you will see how you turned to God. Sure, there may be a lot of other things or people you have turned to, but the bottom line is your faith in God. The bottom line is that He is the only One who has the power and the desire to help you through your difficult time.

In whatever way you are being tested through your child's death, it will not destroy you and it can show where your strength lies. Even though we are silly humans who try to muddle through on our own, the bottom line for each of us is our faith in God; in His love, in His goodness, in His faithfulness, in His mercy, in His ability to rescue us and our families. That is faith.

I know I'm always afraid to say this (1 Corinthians 10:12, *Let him who thinks he stands take heed lest he fall*), but I am encouraged that I am a man of faith. I am encouraged that my son's death did not destroy me, because I turned to the Lord for help. I am encouraged because it has taught me that I know the source of my strength. This should encourage you, too as you think about your journey through grief.

On Your Own:

1 Peter 1:6,7 How is your faith proven? What does this do for you? What is the result of proven faith?

Prayer:

Lord, I thank You that You have not allowed my faith to fail. Help me be encouraged to continue in faith, continue in trust, and even to increase in faith, knowing that because of Your faithfulness to me, I can be faithful to You.

Affirmation:

My faith in God has brought me this far, I continue to walk in faith today.

Got Peace?

You will keep him in perfect peace, whose mind is stayed on You, because he trusts in You.
Isaiah 26:3

There's a lot of things that steal my peace. Hopefully it is always going to be temporary. Peace thieves for me are things like: worry, anxiety, conflict, guilt, shame, trouble, and yes, the worst: tragedy.

So for fun I googled "finding peace." Here's the world's answer:

- 10 things you can start doing today – The Positivity Blog
- 8 things to do if you want to be at peace – Tiny Buddha Blog
- 40 ways to create peace of mind – Tiny Buddha Blog
- 9 ways to find peace of mind in tough times - Planet of Success
- 4 simple steps to peace of mind – Success Blog
- 6 simple steps to find peace within yourself – Huffington Post
- 5 tips to finding peace within yourself – Operation Meditation
- A beautiful method to find POM – Zen Habits
- 5 ways to find peace - Wiki How

These pretty much all fall into four recommendations:
1. Chill out. Relax, don't make mountains out of mole hills, lower your expectations, let go of perfectionism. Let go, accept things for what they are, de-clutter your life.
2. Live in the present. Look forward, not back. Move towards instead of away. Keep short accounts with others, resolve things quickly. Face your struggles, don't numb them or ignore them.

3. Trust yourself. Know yourself, your strengths. Validate yourself.
4. Breathe and Concentrate on peace. Think about peace, perform yoga, enter the "OM zone."

What did Jesus say? *Peace I leave with you, my peace I give to you. I do not give you peace like the world gives. Do not let your hearts be troubled or afraid. I've spoken these things to you so that you may have peace. In the world, you have tribulation, but take courage, I have overcome the world.* John 14:27

There is a definite difference between "attaining" peace and "obtaining" peace. The world's approach to peace is to do all these different things to *attain* peace, to *achieve* peace.

On the other hand, God's peace is given as a gift. It is a gift given in response to our trusting Him, having faith in Him. This is "obtaining" peace.

Attain is something you earn, study for, work for, strive for. *Obtain* is something given to you, granted to you, something you own, something purchased. So, It's one thing to *attain* to the knowledge of peace, or the knowledge of how to achieve peace. It's another thing altogether to actually *obtain* peace, to have peace.

The Bible has a lot to say about peace. 429 times in fact: false peace, inner peace, peace with God, peace with man, peace with myself. Isaiah prophesied: the punishment for our peace & our well-being would fall on Jesus, Messiah. Zachariah prophesied that Jesus would *guide our feet into the way of peace.*

This is possible because (2 Co 5:18-21) Jesus traded places with us: God gave Jesus our sin so that we could have His innocence. In other words, as hard as this may be to believe: Right now God is not counting our wrong-doing against us. He's not mad at us. He's not in heaven licking his pencil and taking notes every time I do something wrong.

This was what Isaiah meant when he said that the punishment for our peace would fall upon Jesus. The Bible says, *He Himself is our Peace.* He is called *the Prince of Peace.*

We can trust Him to work on our behalf in every circumstance, in every trouble. *May the Lord of peace continually grant you peace in every circumstance.* 2 Thessalonians 3:16 *May the God of hope fill you with all joy and peace in believing, so that you may abound in hope by the power of the Holy Spirit.* Romans 15:13

Peace: Confidence in the midst of conflict. The ability to live with yourself. The ability to face God without shame. The ability to face conflict without being conflicted. The ability to face trouble without being troubled. Having confidence in the face of the storm, even in the midst of the storm.

Again, it all boils down to trusting the Lord. Peace is the gift God gives in response to trusting Him.

But how does one trust Him? I had a friend who asked his pastor this question. His pastor said, "Give Him everything. Sit down with a piece of paper and write out everything that is yours, and sign it over to Him, your job, your house, your marriage, your children, everything." That is the path to peace, trust Him with everything.

On Your Own:

Psalm 103:13 Ask yourself, "After all that has happened to me and to my family, can I believe that God is trustworthy?" You, too, may need to write it all out and sign it over to Him.

Prayer:

Lord of all, I am declaring that I trust You. I lay everything important and precious to me at Your feet, and say, "It is Yours." I choose to believe You can and will make it all turn to good. Grant me Your peace. Show me something about Yourself today!

Affirmation:

Today I trust the Lord with _____. (Fill in the blank!)

What Keeps You From Singing?

He who takes shelter in the Most High will abide in the shadow of the Almighty. I will say to the LORD, "My refuge and my fortress, My God, in whom I trust!"
Psalm 91:1

I believe that King David sang more than anybody mentioned in the Bible. King David was also a great warrior. I can't picture a great warrior singing, but most of his writings are songs. Often his songs were about his fears. You would think that a great warrior would be so bold and powerful that fear wouldn't even be in his vocabulary.

Yet you can see over and over in the Psalms that David had many fears. How did he deal with them? Rather than swallow them and push forward, he acknowledged his fears and wrote openly about them. He turned to the LORD and called upon Him. He trusted the Lord for protection and victory.

So often he wrote things like: *Scatter Your enemies, Rout them, Deliver me, Rescue me,* and then he would end his Psalm with, *I will sing a new song to You, O God … To the One who gives victory.* He expresses his fears and his desire for the destruction of the enemy (which for us is death, 1 Corinthians 15:26), and then he expresses his expectation of singing to God for victory when it's all over. Finally, he envisions what life will be like after God's deliverance.

He wrote things like: *Hear, O LORD my cry for mercy, O sovereign LORD, my strong deliverer who shields my head on the day of battle.* He made confessions, like: *I will not be afraid of ten thousands of people who have set themselves against me round about* and, *Even though I walk through the valley of the shadow of death, I fear no evil, for You are with me… and, The LORD is my light and my salvation; whom shall I fear? The LORD is the defense of my life; whom shall I dread* and, *Though a host encamp against me, my heart will not fear.* He made these affirmations in the midst of crying to the LORD about those conspiring against him, those plotting his death, the enemies who sought to destroy him.

Over and over again, throughout the Psalms, we find the mighty King David openly acknowledging his fears and the troubles in his life. He wrote openly of them and expressed them to the LORD in song. He wrote the Psalms to the LORD. They were his confession, his admission of fear and weakness, but also his affirmation of faith and victory. Victory will come through facing and admitting the things that plague us, and then giving them to God and asking Him to be our strength, our victory, our fearlessness, our song.

What are some of the things that keep us from singing? Here's just a few: fear, anger with God, depression, regrets, lack of forgiveness, thoughts of death that eclipse our ability to think beyond it. What are some things that keep you from singing?

On Your Own:

Write out the things that keep you from singing. Just let them flow through your pen. Then offer them up to God and ask Him to carry them for you.

Psalm 59:16,17 In the midst of trouble, why was King David able to sing? Can you find a song in the midst of your trouble? Ask God for a song for today.

Psalm 4:6 When it seems like the world's plan for today is anything but good, what is the solution?

Prayer:

God, I want a song in my heart. Please give me a song for today - maybe though the radio, or through something someone sings or says, or maybe just by bringing one to mind for me. Thank You.

Affirmation:

Today my God is lifting my head high and filling my heart with song.

Verses of Rescue

Many are saying, "There is no deliverance for him in God" but You, O LORD, are a shield about me, my glory and the one who lifts my head.

Psalm 3:3

Even though I walk through the valley of the shadow of death, I fear no evil, for You are with me.

Psalm 23:4

As the deer pants for the water brooks, so my soul pants for You, O God.

Psalm 42:1

Why are you in despair, O my soul? And why have you become disturbed within me? Hope in God, for I shall again praise Him for the help of His presence. O my God, my soul is in despair within me, therefore I remember You.

Psalm 42:5,6

Evening and morning and at noon, I will complain and murmur, and He will near my voice.

Psalm 55:17

You have taken account of my wanderings. Put my tears in Your bottle. Are they not in Your book?

Psalm 56:8

Hear my cry, O God, give heed to my prayer. Lead me to the rock that is higher than I, for You have been a refuge for me, a tower of strength against the enemy.

Psalm 61:1-3

O God, You are my God; I shall seek You earnestly; My soul thirsts for You, my flesh yearns for You in a dry and weary land where there is no water.

Psalm 61:1

Bring my soul out of prison so that I may give thanks to Your name. The righteous will surround me, for You will deal bountifully with me.

Psalm 142:7

Many are saying, "Who will show us any good?" Lift up the light of Your countenance upon us, O LORD! You have put gladness in my heart more than when their grain and new wine abound. In peace I will both lie down and sleep for You, alone, O LORD, make me to dwell in safety.

Psalm 4:6-8

Let all who take refuge in You be glad. Let them ever sing for joy; and may You shelter them that those who love Your name may exult in You. For it is You who blesses the righteous man, O LORD, You surround him with favor as with a shield.

Psalm 5:11,12

Preserve me, O God, for I take refuge in You. I said to the LORD, "You are my Lord; I have no good besides You."

Psalm 16:1,2

Keep me as the apple of the eye, hide me in the shadow of Your wings.

Psalm 17:8

I love You, O LORD, my strength. The Lord is my rock and my fortress and my deliverer, My God, my rock in whom I take refuge; My shield and the horn of my salvation, my stronghold. I call upon the LORD, who is worthy to be praised, and I am saved from my enemies.

Psalm 18:1-3

I would have despaired unless I had believed that I would see the goodness of the LORD in the land of the living.

Psalm 27:13

The LORD is my strength and my shield; My heart trusts in Him, and I am helped. Therefore my heart exults, and with my song I shall thank Him.

Psalm 28:7

Hear, O LORD and be gracious to me; O LORD, be my helper. You have turned for me my mourning into dancing; You have loosed my sackcloth and girded me with gladness, that my soul may sing praise to You and not be silent.

Psalm 30: 10,11

This poor man cried, and the LORD heard him and saved him out of all his troubles. The angel of the LORD encamps around those who fear Him, and rescues them.

Psalm 34:6,7

Light arises in the darkness for the upright. He is gracious and compassionate and righteous.

Psalm 112:4

Precious in the sight of the LORD is the death of His godly ones.

Psalm 116:15

When my soul was overwhelmed within me You knew my path.

Psalm 142:3

When you pass through the waters I will be with you, and through the rivers, they will not overflow you. When you walk through the fire, you will not be scorched, nor will the flame burn you. For I am the LORD your God, the Holy One of Israel, your Savior.

Isaiah 43:2

I will give you the treasures of darkness and hidden wealth of the secret places, so that you may know that it is I, the LORD, the God of Israel, who calls you by name.

Isaiah 45:3,4

He knows the way I take. When He has tried me, I shall come forth as gold.

Job 23:10

Truly, truly I say to you, unless a grain of wheat falls into the earth and dies, it remains by itself alone; but if it dies, it bears much fruit.

John 12:24

This hope we have as an anchor of the soul, a hope both sure and steadfast, and one which enters within the veil, where Jesus has entered as a forerunner for us.

Hebrews 6:19

After you have suffered for a little while the God of all grace, who called you to His eternal glory in Christ, will HIMSELF perfect, confirm, strengthen and establish you.

1 Peter 5:10

When I saw Him I fell at His feet like a dead man. And He placed His right hand on me, saying, "Do not be afraid; I am the first and the last, and the Living One; I was dead, and behold I am alive forevermore, and I have the keys of death and of Hades."

Revelation 1:17,18

He who has an ear, let him hear what the Spirit says to the churches: To him who overcomes, I will grant to eat of the tree of life which is in the Paradise of God.

Revelation 2:7

About the Authors

Whether it's embracing a goat in India, inviting a homeless man over for a shower or just loving on those around them, John and Lynda do it with courage and compassion. Their mantra is to receive life, live life, and give life.

As a Registered Nurse Lynda has done it all: treating bear maulings in Alaska, giving tsunami relief in India, delivering babies on remote islands. Her last nine years as an RN were in the field of hospice care. She states: "I used to help people die now I help people live!" Lynda is founder of Heavenly Hope and Healing Conferences and Ministry. Currently she also works and plays in the field of plant based nutrition with the Juice Plus Company.

For most of his career John worked in and with non profits around the world in the areas of planning and management. He is an ordained minister, with a Master's degree in Divinity. He has ministered for the past 12 years in the GriefShare Ministry at his church.

Their life resume includes: married for 42 years, parents to four amazing children (one who resides in heaven), and three photo – hogging grandchildren.

They call Colorado "home" where they hike and bike in the mountains, and when feeling Aboriginal, paddle board the lakes. They currently work with GriefShare, Umbrella Ministries, and Heavenly Hope and Healing.

Please visit their website at www.HeavenlyHopeAndHealing.org

Made in the USA
Middletown, DE
07 April 2019